DEDIC

For my patients: the folk of Eccles, Swinton and even further afield!
It's been a pleasure, an honour and a privilege.
With my Best Wishes.

WITH THANKS

My sincere thanks to the following very talented people.

Patrick Fahy: for wonderful copy editing: patfahy@lineone.net

Jamie Runyan: another super cover: design@reese-winslow.com

Cover Image: Cape Town, istockphoto, Ferran Traite Soler

Other Books By John Behardien

Crack In the Code
Stars' End

The Last Great Gift

Dawn Over Vancouver
All That Time Allows

Final Horizon
Final Request
Final Truth

One Life Many Moments

ONE LIFE
MANY MOMENTS

by

John Behardien

Duncurin
Publishing

Duncurin.com

Copyright © 2016

All Rights Reserved – John Behardien

No part of this book may be reproduced or transmitted in any form or by any means electronic or mechanical, including photocopying, recording, taping or by any information storage retrieval system without the written permission of the publisher.

This is not a work of Fiction!
Available in Paperback and e-Book.

First Published in England MMXVI

Duncurin Publishing
Monton
England

Duncurin.com

ISBN : 978-0-9935169-2-4

Book Design: Moosey

Contents

Chapter I

An Unusual Name

Behardien. It's such an unusual name, and it must have been especially so when my father came to these shores in the late Twenties. Most people have trouble saying it, let alone spelling it, though I am constantly surprised at how very young patients manage this linguistic feat. My sister, when working as a teacher, always marvelled at how her young class managed to get their tongues around the complicated syllables. This was made even harder when she married and her difficult surname was made even harder when she chose Behardien-Mills as her married name. Young mums will present in my surgery with their toddlers and show as much genuine delight as I do when their little ones somehow manage to wrap their tongues around such a difficult word.

Of course, it's rare in England, mainly because it isn't an English name. My English teacher at Eccles Grammar school put his finger on this one day when talking about surnames. He told the class that English surnames have the emphasis on the first syllable. Thus names such as Taylor, Wilson and Roberts all follow this rule. "Yours, however," he told me, "does not follow this rule as it isn't an English name." He was, without doubt, perfectly correct.

I am told that the name is very common in South Africa, where my father was born. It used to be very rare in the UK but you will see the odd one appearing in more recent times. Most Behardiens are of the Muslim religious persuasion, as my father was but more and more these days, you will also see it with 'Christian' first names, like mine. Pronunciation varies a little but tends to be very different in South Africa and, according to my relatives there, it is often pronounced "Bee-Har-Deen".

My mother however, who was English, sought to change this and anglicise it. She would always pronounce it Bee-Har-Dee-En and we have tended to stick with her version. Those who struggle with it, we encourage to break it down in this way to its component syllables and they often nod and say this is what they had been assuming all along. It is also true when people see it written and then have to have a stab at saying it – they always make commendable efforts. Of course it is often misspelt and sometimes quite spectacularly. My father had a bit of a run-in with the gas company who insisted it should be spelt Behasdrain. He corrected it for them on so many occasions, but every time a new bill came in – it would have reverted to Behasdrain. It was only when he got tough, which was an unusual thing for him, and he refused to pay the bill until they corrected it. They did so in pretty short order after this. Even now, people often spell it Behardian and this, of course, is why so many think it's French or Armenian.

My eldest daughter had an active discussion with one of her tutors at Birmingham where she is a student. He insisted that she had no clue as to where its origins were and that his version, (I forget where now, but it wasn't correct), was right. Many have much more imaginative ways of saying it and I often get 'Bannardo', or my favourite 'Bacardi', which I think has a nice ring to it. When I was at medical school in Cardiff some very clever and imaginative twists were made from my name. The most clever was, unfortunately, so rude that I'd better not reveal it within these pages, in case it offends. One that I can reveal, however, is 'Bed Ridden', which while not as clever as the really rude one, is not bad.

Then, there is the matter of my middle name. So many wonder what this might be and how it is pronounced. It is probably harder than my surname. Yehia, I think, is a Muslim name and this would fit with my Dad being a devout follower of this religion. You may have already guessed that my Mum was a devout Christian. More of this later, but I suspect that when the time came to 'Christen' me or register my birth, my Mum put her foot down and insisted on the most prominent forename being 'John' and my Dad, because he was a graceful and tolerant soul, acquiesced as long as 'Yehia' appeared somewhere. Interestingly, my sister Jane has no such middle name and I guess, once again, that this is a Muslim thing.

You may gather that my knowledge of such things is a bit fuzzy. Part of this reason for this is that my Dad died in 1982 and my Mum in 1996, so neither are here to ask. The other point is that my Dad was devout in his religion, somehow managing to pray five times each day as well as work full-time. He never touched alcohol, though he was very happy for friends and neighbours to do so if they wished. His religion was a private thing, between him and his God, and he never felt the need to ram it down others' throats or advertise it in any way. He was also keen, or at least happy, for me and my sister to choose our own faith, and at all times he would emphasise the similarities and areas of agreement among the world's religions. It is also important to see that his main argument was with those who believed in nothing, rather than with those whose views were only slightly different from his own. More of this later, too.

The other fascinating thing is that the minor surgical procedure that is carried out on Muslim and Jewish boys has not been done to me and I surmise that, once again, my Mum put her foot down and in some way talked my Dad out of such a thing. All in all it gives me an unusual set of initials and though I never advertise my middle name it does not even appear on my passport – it was quite useful when I was looking for a cheaply-priced personal number plate, now many years ago!

Anyway, I drift. I was telling you about my surname. The perceptive among you will realise that although there are many Behardiens in South Africa, it is not an African name. I am also told that there is a very wealthy family in that country with the same surname, though, sadly, we are not related. What I can tell you is that the root of the name was changed, years ago, by the authorities there, or the Afrikaners, from the original. Many names were changed in a similar way. So, where does the root come from? In the 17th Century slaves were brought to South Africa from the Far East. These became known as the Cape Malay or Cape Coloureds. My father was descended from this line. It is also true that my Dad would never have described himself as 'Black' any more than he would have described himself as 'White'. His favourite term, which is frowned upon by political correctness these days, was 'coloured' and he never had a problem with it, or indeed with being so described. This, for my Dad, was simply a means of description and he would use it routinely without seeing it, or even the word 'half-caste' as being in any way discourteous. Some months ago Benedict Cumberbatch was apologising for using the term 'coloured'; my Dad would have wondered what all the fuss was about.

To clarify then, my Dad was born in Cape Town, South Africa, overlooking Table Mountain on or around 1910. He would always describe himself as 'coloured' or possibly Cape Coloured or even Cape Malay. When we were children such things were never discussed with us. This is a shame as I think a little knowledge would have helped my sister and I with the turmoil that was about to engulf us as we grew up.

The other tricky ground we need to cross over is the former British Empire. It is not very trendy these days to say anything good about this and we are encouraged to either ignore it or apologise for it at every verse end. We are also encouraged to watch lots of Mel Gibson films where the English in particular behave as absolute rotters to those nice heroes of the film and this is something that tends to stick, a bit like who recovered the Enigma machine! There is also a penchant in Hollywood for casting the baddy as a well-spoken, plummy English guy with a cut-glass accent. Anyway, be this as it may, I need to tell you that although my Dad was not born a Briton, he had nothing but praise for the British and their Empire. Please accept my apologies for those of you who have just thrown your paperback or even Kindle at the dog at this point, but there we are.

In order to understand his point of view, please remember that he grew up in South Africa at the height of apartheid. This meant that neither coloured people, nor black people could eat where they wanted, or marry whom they wanted to marry, or indeed with whom they were in love! I dread to think what would have happened to him in the South Africa of the 1920s if he had had the temerity to try to marry a white person; this too is a side argument. Let's just say that there was segregation at every level. If you wanted a meal, then regardless of how much money you had in your pocket, you would have to make sure the establishment was for 'coloureds' or 'blacks'. Woe betide anyone who tried to wander into the wrong restaurant or barber's shop and so on. My Dad told me that the white Dutch-Afrikaners were particularly cruel. If a coloured or black person did not get off the pavement quickly enough when a white person was coming the opposite way, then they were summarily beaten and had no right of redress.

Perhaps the saddest thing of all is something my dad once said to me about South Africa. He told me that the coloured people were treated appallingly but that even this was nothing compared to how black people were usually treated by the Afrikaners and establishment of the day.

Let's move on again.

CHAPTER II

Empire and Invitation.

Two events intruded on my Dad when he was still a young lad. The first occurred while he was a member of a social club where they played snooker and billiards. One of their members somehow managed to break his cue. He wanted a replacement and ordered it from the greatest manufacturing nation in the world, where only the finest products (I know this will be seen as either quaint or offensive by many of you, but please bear with me) were made and available – and this, of course, was the heart of the Empire itself. They waited weeks and weeks for it to be shipped, quite literally, in those days, from the hub of the Empire – London. Even when he'd been in the UK for many years and when British manufacturing was well into its terminal decline, my Dad would still look for the vital stamp "Made in England" – now so rare as to be a mere curio of a bygone time.

The second event happened in the early 1920s. (1923, I believe) At that time my Dad was a young man. HMS Hood visited Cape Town bay. My Dad told me when I was very young, with great emotion and pride! (Yes, it's true, I assure you!) He told me that everyone, but everyone, ran down to the bay to catch a glimpse of the most powerful and most beautiful 'battleship' that the world had ever seen. Please note this was so much more than simple curiosity. He told me that the prevailing view was as follows: just who could have designed, engineered and built such a powerful and beautiful ship and then sent it for the view of others. I am sure that most of you are thinking that this was simply an attempt by the Empire to intimidate others, but this most certainly was not the perspective from where my Dad saw things. I don't remember that he commented about how he felt when a more modern 'proper' German battleship sank HMS Hood early in the war but, from what I know of him, it is safe to assume that he was as bereft to learn of the event as anyone in Britain.

In any case both these events intruded upon him in an impactful and (he would have said) positive way. This was almost an invitation, an invitation to a better land with better people and better ways of doing things. He never looked back. Most British folk are almost apologetic. We maybe look at football hooligans or maybe have fessed up about 'causing' slavery and other ills of the world. We see films where much cooler, funnier, more brilliant nations have totally eclipsed us with much more trendy language, ideas and practices. My Dad's view was diametrically opposite to this. In any event any of you can read the history books and form your own opinions but his view was simply that the Empire was, by and large, a good thing and the people behind it were fundamentally good, just and fair people, whom he wanted to join and emulate. I am sorry in a way that British people cannot see themselves through his eyes as they could, and should, be very proud of what they would then see. I'll touch on this again later.

In any event, he spent his life trying to be more British, and English in particular. Most vitally this was his approach; he was grateful to have been accepted by such wonderful people and to have the chance of a better way of life; one that was without fear or persecution – where one could be what one wanted to be. He wasn't about importing a little piece of where he had come from; his life was all about becoming part of the whole. He would have hated the modern tendency of people labelling themselves as British Muslim. He would have wanted to say British, and his religion was a private thing, between him and God.

When he was seventeen his Mum (his Dad had died by this time) committed all their funds to sending him to the Empire itself and, perhaps, not that far from the yard that had built HMS Hood; in fact to Edinburgh University, to study Medicine. In Edinburgh he was quite simply amazed; although he never got out of the habit of calling everyone he met "Sir", he was greeted as an individual and as an equal. Okay, I am sure there were many people who perhaps were bigoted but, by his accounts, not many. Moreover, he was able to go in any restaurant and provided he had the money, he could eat: same with the barbers. The Scottish people impressed him by their acceptance of him, their willingness to teach and the wonderful institutions like Universities, Banks and Hospitals that, of course, they still have in place today. In a further inflammatory statement, which really will have some of you throwing your Kindle at the dog, I can say that my Dad held the view that the Scottish and the English were a powerful and mutually-supportive partnership.

After qualifying, he moved to England but, before this, World War 2 got in the way. There was never any question of his not wanting to be involved. The fight of Britain and the Empire was also his fight. He wanted to sign up to fly Spitfires but they would not let him do that; as soon as they found out he had a medical qualification they enlisted him in the Royal Army Medical Corps. He would tell me about the long lines of troops, needing inoculations. He would have one syringe and one needle. They would jostle to be the first, not because of the risks of cross infection, that would get a doctor struck off today if he or she used a needle or syringe more than once, but simply because this was when the needle was at its sharpest and least painful. He told me that it was not unusual for men to faint, especially if they were at the back of the line. I still have a little glass cylinder that contains a carousel or a rack of some of his glass syringes. The needles were very long and very thick. They did not have disposable needles in those days and presumably, after use, they were either boiled or put in an autoclave using superheated steam to 'sterilise' and, when blunt, they would be sent for service to be re-sharpened and then returned to the doctor. Please note also that neither boiling nor even the autoclave has been shown to be one hundred per cent effective, unlike modern sterilising techniques and, as you will have seen, the current trend is to use only single-use syringes, needles, speculae and so on.

After the war, he moved to Manchester in the 1950's. He went home just the once to tell his family that he was getting married, to my Mum whose family come from Goostrey, I believe. She was one of five daughters. Diamonds were plentiful in South Africa in certain areas.

Massive corporations controlled very carefully (and still do!) the supply, marketing, desirability and therefore price of what Dad told me were to be found on the ground in certain areas. You would be shot (black or white!) if you tried to enter those areas. He bought a large diamond while he was there and smuggled it out in a large pot of jam. In those days South Africa would export things like fruit and preserved fruit in large containers almost like oil cans. My Dad smuggled the diamond for an engagement ring for our Mum. My sister has this ring today.

As soon as he was settled in Monton, his pro-English stance moved up a gear. Of course in those days one could only buy British cars, but as the Japanese and Germans started to make inroads, he would still prefer to buy British. Indeed, when out shopping with my mum, he would often turn things over to see where they were made. If the stamp was 'Made in England' or 'Great Britain' he would purchase the item or, otherwise, do without. I am sorry if this sounds rather quaint these days, but this is the man he was and those are the forces that had shaped him. Most importantly he was grateful to be in a country where he felt comfortable and secure; and although his religion remained a private thing, he would put his country (ie Great Britain) first and all other issues were secondary. Each day of his life he aspired to be more British and was proud to do so. Seems a long time ago somehow.

Although there was a large Yemeni community in Eccles, I suspect that a mixed marriage was a pretty rare thing, even at the end of the 1950s when my sister and I were born. One reads about countries today where such things are discouraged with vehemence. Even the pillar of coolness and forward thinking, the USA, has a great many problems in such areas that still make unfortunate news.

My Dad had set up his surgery in our home, on Monton Green just facing the Blue Bell. There are still one or two patients from that time who can remember me as a little boy riding round the waiting room on my little trike. The poor patients, who were no doubt feeling unwell, would have to continually move their feet as I cycled round and round. One unfortunate lady got so fed up with this that she got hold of the trike and quickly shunted me out of the waiting room!

My Dad took lots of cine footage from this time and it shows my sister and me as young children in the back garden and on Monton Green. Our mum was always keen that we should be well turned out and my sister, Jane, in particular always had a dress on with a matching bow in her hair. We were regular visitors to the shops in Monton and just a few months ago I met the daughter of the couple who kept the greengrocer's. There is also much footage of me as a baby being pushed by my sister up and down the steep path at break-neck speed; me sitting oblivious to the dangers not in my pram but in her toy pram!

It wasn't my Mum's first marriage. She'd been married some years before, but sadly her husband died and she'd been left with a little boy, Rodney, to bring up on her own. These things are more common these days but back then it must have been hard going. She told me once that Rodney had become very ill. This was before the NHS and she scraped the money together in order to get a doctor to come. The doctor diagnosed diphtheria and advised her that he would definitely not survive the night. Rodney had other ideas. He was off school for such a long time but mercifully survived. He didn't get any qualifications from school as he had been off so long. He never let this hold him back, however, and he attended night school and eventually gained accountancy qualifications. I don't think he has had a day off sick ever since. He is twenty-one years older than me and as I was growing up Rodney was either working or doing National Service and shortly after got married and moved, at first to Prestwich, then London, then South Africa and then Cyprus. We used to love him visiting with his family as he used to always take us to exciting places, like the fun-fair at Southport. One Christmas he took us to the toy-fair in Kendals and I don't remember a more magical Christmas. A more enthusiastic and hard-working person I have never met; so much so he refuses to retire and still has lots of clients in Cyprus and around the world.

When I was a young lad, Dad would love to watch cricket and, you'll have guessed, always supported England. I remember he was amazed when a cricketer from South Africa, who was also a Cape Coloured, was picked for England. Basil D'Oliveira was a middle-order batsman and could also do a bit of bowling. I remember my Dad saying one day when Basil walked to the crease to take up position. "This could never have happened in South Africa." But of course it did in the fullness of time and I am sorry my Dad didn't live to see the changes that have been made in his country of birth. Although I have never been to South Africa many of my patients holiday there and tell me what a wonderful country it is today.

CHAPTER III

Accidents

This brings me on nicely to something, certainly at an early age of a charmed existence. I don't think it would be true to say that I was a naughty boy. Until the age of six, I was very quiet. Unfortunately I managed to get myself into a string of potentially serious situations. All of these were life-changing and most of them would also have been life-threatening. Although I am not someone who has won raffles or competitions, the occasions that I have needed a little luck were the times when it did not desert me. To say that I had nine lives would not have been an exaggeration.

The first took place when I was very young. I had learned to ride my tricycle and was going round the back garden. All the houses on Monton Green had large cellars, in our case this is where our central heating boiler was located, and the coal stores. There were some outside stone steps that led down via a full flight to some doors, which could be opened for the coal man to bring the sacks of coal. The top of these steps was protected by a little swing gate. My mum says that she was in the kitchen and saw me cycle past her window. I then crashed into the gate, which promptly opened and I went down, still on my tricycle, the full flight of stone steps. She came rushing out of the house to see me sitting at the bottom a bit shaken, presumably, but otherwise unhurt.

I was also very young when I nearly electrocuted myself for the first time. In those days sockets were not like the magnificent and safe ones that we have now, which I believe are the best in the world. In those days they were round and had three holes, the middle one was the earth and there were two 'live' ones either side. Our lounge had one such socket. Modern ones also have 'shutters' which seal off the live holes until and unless the long earth prong from the plug goes in. As this happens, the shutter is released and the plug can access the two live holes. Sockets in those days had no such shuttering; they were a perfect size for children's fingers to poke into or for little fingers to get round the partially inserted or withdrawn plug. My fingers were ideal for this and it wasn't long before I tried it out. Please remember, too, that houses in those days didn't have circuit breakers like they all do nowadays. If one was lucky the fuse would blow but this would be long after one had been electrocuted. In went my fingers and although I don't remember I am told I was thrown across the room by the force of the shock. Sadly, I suspect that I was not the only one to attempt this. Some years later the plugs and sockets that we recognise today were introduced. I wonder occasionally just how many paid a high price before they were brought in.

For my next trick as a little boy, I sneaked into my Dad's surgery and found a batch of slimming tablets and promptly ate them all. At the time slimming tablets were very much in vogue and were based on Amphetamine derivatives. They were very dangerous to adults in overdose and especially to young children. An Ambulance was promptly called as soon as my Mum and Dad realised what I'd done. I was rushed to casualty at Hope Hospital where doctors and nurses each held down a leg or an arm while my stomach was pumped out. I survived and was kept in overnight. It strikes me that a significant delay would have brought about a very different outcome. This type of slimming tablet has been banned long ago, simply because they were just too dangerous!

Then there was the time when my mum was ironing in the kitchen. Irons in those days were very heavy. I was crawling round the kitchen floor and managed to pull the hot iron on to my face. I am amazed that I was not permanently scarred by such a thing. The other point is that with so many accidents happening to one little boy, these days Social Services would be alerted and safeguarding meetings would be set up. Then there was the time we had a few friends round for a birthday party. I must have been a few years old. We had some picnic tables with detachable legs. My Mum was packing away and whisked one of these upwards. It caught me just below my left eye. You can see the 1cm scar there to this day. A few millimetres upward and it would have taken my eye out.

We had a little cottage at Bull Bay, Anglesey. Mum and Dad would often invite family to travel with them for a weekend or a few days. Uncle Jim and Aunty Audrey came with us once with their son Martin who was a little older than I was. Uncle Jim was a 'scout leader' sort of person with a big moustache and a penchant for woodbines. One day, he took Martin and me for a fishing trip along the cliffs. Photos of him remind me of those mountaineers who went up mountains and polar caps with just a woollen fleece and a tin of baccy. We perched on a rocky outcrop way above the sea and I glanced down at the rough, cold and unforgiving waves below. We dangled our long lines down and sat there. A few minutes later a sea lion popped its head out of the water and then, after a quick curious glance, submerged again. I remember thinking, 'gosh, I wouldn't like to fall from here.' Suddenly I was off the edge and heading for the waves. Of course I could not swim. Down I went straight for those cold waves forty feet below. Miraculously what could not be seen from the top was a hidden shelf that was a couple of metres below my position. Somehow I landed on this on my back, a bit winded and very shaken but otherwise still on terra firma. Uncle Jim and Martin pulled me up. I told Martin that I could not swim and he told me that I wasn't to worry; Uncle Jim would have dived in to rescue me. I was not at all sure about this. I think if I'd gone in, I would have drowned that day.

We had an old radiogram in the attic. This was a very large valve-operated radio complete with record deck and built in amplifier and speakers. Many of you will be aware that this old valve-operated equipment ran very high voltages and also very high currents. It was also a perfect source of my second brush with electricity. As a very curious little boy I was poking around the back of it one day and discovered this little wire, which of course I pulled. The electric shock threw me across the room for the second time. My sister heard me cry out and asked me if I was okay. I told her that I'd just stumbled and fallen, not being keen to draw attention to yet another life-threatening accident.

As an older boy I would often play with my friends and we'd play with soldiers, tanks and aircraft. I remember the Captain Scarlet range of SPV – Spectrum Pursuit Vehicle and MSV – Maximum Security Vehicle were very popular as were Action Men and so on. In those days you could buy penny bangers in the shops. I think these came in packs of four or five. The trick was to light them and then throw them, which is probably why they no longer sell them! Older boys would show you how to break them open and release the gunpowder inside which would make for a much bigger and more impressive 'explosion'. I calmly took my plastic model of a Lancaster bomber and was intent in creating an authentic crash scene, mercifully in the garden. I poured on to the wings the contents of four bangers and then promptly set it off. As you will all realise the gunpowder went off with quite an explosion and my face was in close proximity. In quite an instructive lesson to me I could not see and went staggering round the garden for many minutes, wondering if my sight would return.

I'm sure you all realise, just as I did in that moment that there is a fine line between delight, excitement, danger and disaster. I wonder how close I came to the latter that day. After what seemed like an age but cannot have been more than 5 minutes my sight returned. Once again luck had saved me from abject stupidity and often in the news one comes across sad cases of young boys in particular not being as lucky as I was. Without doubt another humbling experience for me. There was worse, much worse to come. I'll save the most horrific accident for another chapter.

It seems my sister and I both had a penchant for the dangers of electricity. I remember some years later we moved house. In point of fact we moved next door, from number ten Monton Green to number eight. Jane realised that we had not brought the lamp that was in our morning room. She went to get it but discovered that our Dad had wired it directly into the socket and it could thus not be disconnected. She calmly went to the kitchen and found a bread knife with which she proceeded to cut the live cable. Mercifully she rejected the metal scissors and took the knife instead. For many years we kept that bread knife but it had a permanently etched flash burn on its cutting edge and also a great cavity where the metal had been melted by the flash and the 'explosion' of shorting mains current. The miracle of it was that although the knife had a wooden handle the metal blade ran between the wooden halves of said handle and there were two metal rivets that went right through the handle to keep it all together. I am happy to report that she was completely unscathed but on many occasions we would look at that knife and think of less appealing outcomes.

CHAPTER IV

Family Disasters

Disasters were not just confined to us two kids. Our Mum and Dad seemed to have a few of their own.

One day my Dad was on call and reversed down the drive in our Ford Anglia to go and do some visits. The rear window was open and somehow from the washing line he managed to pick up a pair of knickers which must have flapped behind the car as he went off to do his rounds. I remember he always wore a fedora-type hat and was quite strait-laced. I am not sure what his patients thought when he turned up with a pair of knickers flapping in the breeze behind him.

In time the solid-fuel boiler was replaced by an oil-fired one. In the cellar a large 1,000 gallon tank was welded in place. Every few months they would come with supplies of fuel oil. One day they somehow managed to connect the fuel tanker to the wrong pipe and the whole cellar was flooded with 1,000 gallons of fuel oil. Within minutes another tanker appeared squirted the whole cellar to capacity with special foam and then sucked the whole thing clear.

My Dad had lots of Yemeni patients on his list. They could appear at just about any time. One Sunday one such appeared. Dad was out on rounds and it must have been about 2 pm. My Mum asked the gentleman to wait in the waiting room. At about 11 pm mum and dad were off to bed. A little cough came from the waiting room that had been in darkness for some hours. The poor chap was still there! My Dad saw to him and he was on his way by 11:20 pm. My Mum had forgotten all about him! I wonder what would happen if this scenario was played out today.

Mum also told me about the time that they were journeying to Anglesey. They were hopelessly lost and stopped a squaddie to ask for directions. He told them that he knew exactly where they were headed and jumped in the back and offered to take them. He took them all over the Island, promptly got out at his base. They asked him about their destination and he then said that he had no idea where that was and walked off.

Apparently many years ago cars were not fitted as standard with windscreen wipers. My Dad's new car had been in to the local dealer to have these fitted. It came back from the dealership and it was put away in our little garage. That night a terrible fire started and both car and garage were incinerated. The garage discovered that the wiring to the wipers had been faulty and this had caused the fire. Thirty years later my Dad wondered if it might have been the little paraffin heater he had in there so that the car would start in all weathers. He wondered if it was this that had started the fire. Some things are better not known.

Their little cottage in Anglesey was, at that time, before they built housing estate, overlooking the sea near Bull Bay. Dad bought a pair of binoculars. These were magnificent things and on much of the cine footage you will see Jane, or me as young children carrying these. They also came in a superb leather case which was lined. My Dad discovered with horror that the case was made from pig skin. He spent the next hour covering the case in polythene and then painstakingly wrapped the pig skin strap in cellotape so that he did not come into contact with it directly. As a little boy I asked my Mum what Dad was doing with his new binoculars and she told me that he did not like the material that covered the case and this was why he was carefully covering it all.

One of my favourite incidents was the time when my Mum was driving through Eccles in the Ford Anglia. Another driver cut her up and she was anxious to give him a piece of her mind. She wound her window down and shouted to him, "Where are your L-plates?" Her car must have moved forward a little as he shouted back just as she remembered that my sister was learning to drive, "Oh, I see you've got yours on!" I wonder how different the interaction between two upset drivers would be today.

Then there was the time that Jane visited our aunt who had a shop in Peel Green. Jane had just learned to drive and Mum had a Hillman Imp. Sabre, our family dog of which more later, was in the back and had gone along, as was his wont, for the ride. Unfortunately as she turned right out of Alexandra road a speeding car hit her and demolished the car. She was unhurt but all the windows were broken. The terrified dog jumped out and then went missing. We went searching for him and spent hours just travelling round. We asked everyone if they had seen him and so many came to help us. The following morning we found him on the fields at the back of Gorton Street, looking a bit dishevelled and very hungry but otherwise very pleased to see us.

I remember many years ago an incident that upset my mum. It was raining heavily and she was driving through Ellesmere Park. Two schoolgirls were sheltering under a tree and she'd stopped to offer them a lift. They in turn had become upset and run off. This was the time of Myra Hindley and Ian Brady and children had had it drummed into them never to get into a stranger's car. She told me some time later that she felt very foolish, though of course trying to be helpful. Apparently both girls were drenched. Dad said she should not have approached them in this way – a sad reflection of modern times.

Probably the worst one was, again, all, my fault. The four of us together with a friend of Emmie's had all been skiing in Canada. We were due to fly back via Calgary airport. We got to the airport in good time and put our bags through. As we walked to the gate I saw on the screen that our flight had 'Update in 18:00', which was about 2 hrs off. I then heard a man say that there were winds over the Atlantic and his flight to Gatwick had been delayed. We sat down to wait thinking our flight was delayed. Crucially, we sat just outside the gate as exactly the same thing had happened one winter in Geneva where the flight was re-arranged and a new gate was given so that we'd had to come out of the gate and go through security once again. I kept checking the board and on the intercom were lots of notices for people to move their cars and so on. I checked every few minutes but the screen did not change. I walked back to the check-in and there were all new people there who could tell me nothing. I looked again at the screen and I saw that out flight had disappeared completely. I asked the lady what this meant and she said that this meant that the flight had gone. She picked up the phone and said that they were desperately trying to get our bags off so that they could depart. What had saved us was the fact that our bags were in the hardest part of the hold to reach. We rushed to the gate where the lady told me that they had been waiting for us for two hours. She shouted at me as to how I could have been so stupid. I told her as I stood there that I was happy to receive more of her shouting but it might be best if she simply let us through so that the flight could get under way. I asked why if they had been waiting for us that they did not simply Tannoy us? She told me that Calgary was a silent airport. We got on the plane and everyone clapped. We were so embarrassed. I could have died with shame.

There were 400 people on that flight. I sat in my chair and did not move apart from one trip to the toilet in 9 hours. The stewardess came to ask me what had happened for her report and I told her about my mistake. She was very nice and said I would not be the first, nor the last person to delay a transatlantic flight. On the way back there was a magnificent view of the Aurora Borealis, but I did not dare leave my seat to take a look! Whenever we fly these days we always make sure we go straight to the gate and Frankie tells me that she still has nightmares about this incident.

As always, what came next was the most interesting. I wrote to Monarch to apologise and also to ask them which charity they supported. I sent a cheque to Macmillan nurses for £400, a pound for each person on the flight. The lady at Monarch wrote to thank me and also apologised for the lady who shouted at me. I told her that I deserved it. She then wrote back to say that she had worked for 29 years she had never experienced anyone apologise for causing a flight to be delayed. I think this is very sad, although, of course, it didn't really atone for my stupidity. We are all still very nervous fliers these days even though it is some years ago!

Finally, our Dad also had a bit of an uneasy relationship with electricity. At Christmas time he would always make sure that we had a festive tree with lights on it. There would be a big box of such lights in the cellar and he would spend an hour untangling all the wires before finally putting them on the tree. I'm told that his and Jane's favourite were so called 'bubble lights' which had a hot-running bulb in the base and featured a little glass tube which when heated would bubble satisfyingly. With the passage of time these became more and more erratic and one Christmas we had a lucky escape when the whole tree nearly went up! Never, ever leave a Christmas tree on if you go out!

My favourite, however, was the immersion timer that he fitted in the bathroom so that the water would be hot when he got up at the crack of dawn to pray. The timer was mains-wired but the wire went all along the bathroom wall where it was tacked by clips but above the bath! Our Mum put her foot down and said the whole thing looked so unsightly and had to go. Mercifully, he took it down before anyone was electrocuted in the bath!

Chapter V

School

I was not at all keen on school. I started at the age of three and met my friend Robin on the first day. We were at a small private school. In some ways this was a bit of a gentle start to school life, but as I will discuss appearances could be deceptive. At the end of the first day I informed my mum that it wasn't bad but I thought that I would not go again. She told me that if I didn't go to school, then the policeman would come and tell both her and my Dad off and things would go badly for them. I went to school from this point and, having accepted my fate, loved it from that day onwards. Lots of the kids were Jewish and bussed down from Prestwich. We were at school with sons and daughters from many of the large businesses in Prestwich. Not that at that age we were aware of any differences whatsoever. My sister and I were the only coloured kids in the school. Again not that anyone knew any different.

In some ways the place was ruled with a rod of iron. Even a minor transgression would attract a punishment. One lunchtime I was pushed out of the queue for the bathroom. I was doing my best to push my way back in when Mr Firth, the headmaster saw me and immediately took me down to the cloakrooms for a good hiding from his oversize slipper that he kept for such occasions. Nobody was allowed to swear. If any swear words were heard then the offender would literally have his or her mouth washed out with soap and water. I remember Callum Mackenzie, who was the son of Dr Forbes Mackenzie, came out with what was reported to be, "Damn" one day and he was whisked off for the mouth-scrubbing treatment. In addition, at lunch, we were not allowed to leave any food at all. To this day I shudder at the sight of butter beans and mashed potato and overcooked swede. Large vats would contain the sickly yellow stuff and the lumpy mashed potato and my dietary nemesis – the butter beans. I used to retch at the sight of the butter beans. I knew that I simply could not eat them. To refuse or to be sick would attract an even worse punishment: more of this later. One kid put salt on someone else's food. His own plate was removed and replaced with one covered in salt. When he was sick he was told to clean it all up and then get back to class.

Although I was by no means a very clever little boy, I did have an active imagination and a brain that would generate good ideas. On many occasions this would get me out of trouble. Mercifully, at these dark times where there was a pile of steaming butter beans in front of me, I struck on an idea. Many of my friends had trouble eating dumplings. I didn't mind these so much. I therefore suggested a trade whereby I would eat their dumplings if they ate my butter beans. Provided we were quick and not seen, this arrangement worked well. To this day I cannot stomach them, even the smell makes me come over in a sweat. Moreover, mashed potato is not a favourite and if offered this at a dinner party I struggle with it manfully but make sure I am not given too much and leave what seems polite. My sister, Jane, has a similar antipathy towards mash. Frankie, my wife, and our girls love mashed potato and if she is cooking this she always whips some whole potatoes out of the pan before she mashes them up. Why anyone would wish to smash potatoes in this way is lost on me though curiously I don't mind potato cakes with a bit of butter on them.

I was, as you'll see shortly, left-handed. It is said that left handers are more creative and I think I was destined to be a quiet, dreamy sort of little boy who would have been content to drift a little through life and my left-handed preference would have brought out my more arty, touchy-feely side. This was unacceptable to the school of the day. We began writing with chalk and a small slate. Naturally, I picked the chalk up with my left hand. As soon as I did so, however, the teacher came and smacked the back of my wrist with a ruler. Eventually after getting a very sore wrist I decided to go with the flow and attempt to write with my right. This was to have significant consequences later when I was aged eleven.

My other horror was, without doubt, swimming lessons. We used to go to the baths along Cromwell Road. Each week I swallowed more and more pool water. The headmaster used to hold me under the water and I was terrified. Everyone, the whole school, had learned to swim a length and I couldn't manage a width. I was the swimming laggard of the whole school. Each week I would have to stay in the water longer and longer while the others could get out and get changed. Each week I would fail. Much worse, however, was my strategy to try to make an excuse each Friday – any sort of reason why I could not go swimming. Surely avoiding my deepest fears was the best way through? More of this later, too. It seemed I used to petition my Dad for a note to say that I wasn't well. Once my sister closed the bathroom door on my toe, which immediately started bleeding and the nail came up at an awkward angle. I was delighted because it meant no swimming for a few weeks. The headmaster was very angry and called me to the front of the class where he asked me to take my shoes and socks off so as to show everyone.

The other point about swimming and games was that when you got dressed you could not leave until or unless you had tied your school tie. This for some was very difficult and some would help others providing the headmaster was not around. Mercifully I learned this skill fairly quickly though I suspect at school I was a bit of a dullard. My sister was far cleverer and had a much quicker mind than mine. Our Mum said that she started walking at ten months and developed language skills much quicker than I did. She could tie her tie in no time and of course in summer the girls had their summer dresses.

Coming back to the swimming - sooner or later I just had to face my fear. I had run out of excuses and felt really panicky inside. I could run from it no longer. This realisation stood me in good stead for the rest of my life. Each week the whole school, who had been allowed to vacate the pool and get dressed, would peep over the cubicle doors that surround the pool of the old Eccles baths to this day. I would be struggling so much that I was convinced that I was going to drown in that pool. Some of the older kids had certificates for swimming a mile, including my sister. I could not even stay afloat.

One day, however, it struck me that it was having my face in the water that I hated. This in turn made me frightened that I would not be able to breathe. I asked the headmaster if I could attempt backstroke, which I had never done before. Most crucially, this meant I could breathe when I wanted and my face was out of the water. At first I held my body tense with fear and this caused it to bend in the middle so that I started to sink. I then realised that by actually stretching out in the water and pushing my head up a little my face stayed out of the water and away I went. All the kids in the cubicles held their breath as they got changed, watching my latest attempt. Somehow I managed to get to the end. The whole school cheered. I had swum a length! The headmaster was delighted and picked me out of the water and held me aloft. When he presented my 'length' certificate in assembly one morning, he told the school about how I had not realised how far I had gone until my head hit the end wall and once again they all cheered. I didn't become a swimmer overnight. Even to this day I am nervous about swimming without my goggles and whenever getting out of my depth.

They closed Eccles baths some years ago and today it is the Link Centre. I remember in the vestibule just outside the baths there would be a hot drinks machine. Occasionally I would have sixpence, note the old currency. On putting this in the machine one could choose coffee or more interestingly hot chocolate which wasn't very nice or chicken noodle soup, which was amazing. Most weeks I was either lagging so much behind or had no money so I could not try it. However on the odd occasion that I was able to do so it tasted divine. Many, many years later one of the attendees at the Link centre became poorly. They asked if one of the local GPs would visit. I was asked to go. I got there and went inside. It has changed somewhat but much of what I remember remains. Most notably, as I went in through the doors I could smell that chicken noodle soup.

Although still being a hopeless swimmer, I had done enough for now to keep the headmaster at bay and I think I must have left the school before I was required to do more certificates. As a young doctor, I found a class that offered private swimming lessons in Prestwich. There I was at the age of twenty-three with water wings on. I would often pop and see my sister at her house when I had finished my lesson. Her husband would ask me if I was going to come inside. I would politely decline saying that I had swallowed so much water and that I felt so sick that I had better not! Eventually I got through the course and though I am still not a strong swimmer I do manage to swim at my gym twice a week, though I am usually exhausted after spending an hour in the gym beforehand and soon collapse in the Jacuzzi. One lady just this week told me that I looked like an experienced swimmer with a good action in the water. I can only think she was joking!

More troubles awaited all of us at school. One little boy, who was the son of Mr Ellbaum, a consultant orthopaedic surgeon, fell in the playground. He returned to class saying that he could not write, as his wrists were hurting. The headmaster told him to get on with his work. When he was a bit reluctant to do this because of the pain he was taken down to the cellar and given the slipper. This happened again when he said he was in too much pain. After school his father took him into Casualty at Crumpsall where his wrists were X-rayed and both were found to be broken. He came in the following day with both wrists in plaster.

Unsurprisingly, I was always anxious to keep under the radar where possible and not attract any attention. Unfortunately little boys are subject to temptation. One of my friends threw leaves over me in the playground. I responded by throwing some on him. The headmaster witnessed this and came rushing outside to inform us that we were both on detention and were required to stay behind after school to sweep the playground. We would then go outside school to sweep Clarendon Crescent and when we had done that we'd finish with Victoria Crescent. I often drive along these roads today and think what long roads they are. They were certainly a lot longer to a little boy. My Mum came to pick me up at 3:30 and was told I was on detention. She came back at 5 pm for me and we were still sweeping. She asked the headmaster if he had ever been a little boy? I was told I could go. I am not sure how long the other boy, Jeremy, was required to stay.

Despite the harsh conditions the school was academically advanced and although I was by no means at the top of the class I was taught lots of stuff especially in Mathematics and English – and very quickly. I had a bit of an interest in Mathematics and one night we were given homework to do which comprised two pages, mainly addition and subtraction, of tens and units and hundreds, tens and units. I somehow misheard what the teacher said and rather than go back in with the homework not done – which was not advised, I finished the whole book. This was one of those stories that went round the whole school.

Sadly, or otherwise, it was not to last. My sister went to senior school and at the same time one of our friends, who was I think the year below me, was in deep trouble. She was unable to eat the food. She started out on first-sitting for lunch. She could not eat. She was then required to sit through second-sitting and still could not eat. She was then placed in the garage and remained there. The poor girl would fill her pockets with the food in an attempt to get rid of it. At each stage of the way she was given the slipper. After some days of this she went home and at bath time her mum discovered that she was covered in large bruises. You must remember that in those days the headmaster had ultimate authority. This is why so many Jewish kids came down from Prestwich because their parents held the view that Mr Firth could mete out punishments that they could not. At that time, however, the girl's parents decided to take action against the school. My Dad was her GP and was asked to provide a medical report. He did so but thought it best if I move from the small private school to a local state school, Clarendon Road. I must have been about aged nine. This was a big shock and although there was no slipper and no requirement to eat all the food, other problems awaited me.

I was given more than a hint of what awaited me a year or two before. I'd been saving my pocket money for weeks and was then allowed to buy the little car from the toyshop in Monton. A man called Mr Williams kept the toyshop and I think it must have been where the Drop Inn and more lately the Blind Pig is located. I asked my Mum if I could go up the road and over the other side, where I had found the pavement to be particularly smooth. The roads were fairly quiet in those days in Monton. She asked me to be careful crossing the main road at the top and off I went. I ran all the way up Monton Green and over the road at the top. If I could go back in time, I would want to go back and stop that little boy. I would want to talk to him so much. He was for sure a quiet and unassuming little chap who was not loud, disruptive or naughty – perhaps a little. I would want to stop him and simply say to him that he was to do his best to be very brave that day and that he was going to be all right. Please note I would not stop him from going, nor would I ask him to run back to his mummy.

I was flicking my little Corgi racing car up and down the pavement. Suddenly, a lady came charging out of one of the houses. She must have seen me running up and down the pavement. She looked very angry, but also strangely worried and almost frightened. I remember to this day what she said as she shouted questions at me in rapid succession.

"What are you doing? Where have you come from? Where do you live? What are you doing here?"

I pointed down the road towards Monton Green. I said that I was playing with my little car and that I lived in one of the houses down there. She retained her anger and said, "I don't want your sort playing round here, now go back home at once! Never come back here. I don't want to see your sort round here – ever."

I grabbed my little car and ran back home at once. The racing car was a Lotus and it must have been the early 1960's. I was about six. I have an almost identical one in my glass cabinet in my surgery to this day but I never played with that little car again.

As I said, I would love to be able to go back and talk to that little boy. If I had a time machine I would go back as he ran back down the road, his little heart so worried and so sad. I'd stop him and tell him that, yes things had changed, but he'd come through and most crucially this woman was in the minority. I was a quiet, unassuming little boy who, had it not been for that incident would have drifted through life in a more or less carefree manner. People say that children cannot see very much and do not understand the nuances of complex emotion as expressed by adults. I would beg to differ.

I wondered what it was about her that had caused her to say these things to a little boy. I knew too that my life would be different from this point on. I knew that she had judged me purely on my appearance, and she did not like what she saw. She seemed frightened of having me in front of her house and obviously did not wish to have me, or a person like me, anywhere near. It was almost as though she saw me as a threat or even as some sort of pollutant.

I knew that if I told my Mum, she would have gone up there and ripped her head off. I knew, also, that my Dad would be very upset. I realised that my life had changed that day. In some ways my quiet and carefree childhood had ended and new forces were now in place. I knew that I could never be at the mercy of someone who would judge me harshly purely on a glance. Having judged me they would then disadvantage me by default. I knew, too, that I had to face my difficulties alone. You may wonder why I said that I would not stop that little boy from running up the road and having his heart broken. The simple answer is that that woman made me. The changes I began to put in place that day assured success at school, in learning and also whenever things got bad and I had to face the fear. A fire started burning within that I was no longer able to extinguish. I sometimes read about these really successful fund managers. Many of the really successful ones are from broken homes or ones who never knew their parents. I remember reading about one whose father had disowned him and he'd been fostered. Years later when he was now worth billions, his natural father contacted him. He told him that he had a father (his foster dad) and that he wasn't really welcome.

I guess my view is that at times in our lives when the comfortable existence is threatened or altered, we have a choice. We can either put in the changes that are needed and step up or we can continually run from it. I knew that hiding from difficulties and unpleasantness would only make them worse. I guess instinctively I knew that I had to grasp the nettle or spend the rest of my days in a state of continual fear.

Of course, everyone these days has stories of how they were bullied at school. I am sure too that every person with a 'coloured' skin will have one or two similar. I am no exception. I think we were the only such family in Monton at that time. One of my patients who is from Ireland told me that someone at work once told him that all Irish people should go back to Ireland! I suspect too that for many who are a little different this is at the milder end of the spectrum.

Ultimately, this angry and fearful woman caused me to change. I knew I had to achieve. I became somebody different that day and put in the changes that I needed. Even today after such a long journey and facing the trials that I have, I am attempting to find the person that that little boy would have become. What is not in doubt as things stood there and then, I had to be in a position where others could not subject me purely to their mercy – nor judge me solely by how I looked. School was to be my vehicle and hard work would be the thing that fuelled me. A hunger stirred inside me, to be the best that I could possibly be at school. There started a thirst to put in as much work as was required to place me in those top spaces at school and this continued until I went to University at eighteen and beyond.

Nobody at the private school swore or used bad words. I was naïve as to most naughty words anyway. My parents didn't swear. My mum who, as I said, was a devout Christian used the odd 'damn!' but that was about it. As soon as I got to Clarendon Road, however things changed within days. I was subjected to a barrage of swear words, none of which I understood. Thinking it was best to try to fit in I took them all up pretty quickly and, it has to be said, I did not understand any of them. It was a painful lesson – never use words you don't understand!

Sadly, for me, I picked up on 'Coon' and 'Wog' very quickly and as they sounded cool started saying these to my classmates. One of them told me that I was not to call him these names as it meant a dark person. I realised in the moment just why I had heard them so frequently. Others then came thick and fast. One little boy, who still lives locally, had a penchant for saying,

"Go black, home, you'll be all white tomorrow." And another that he was particularly delighted with "Where are you from Niggereria?" Only some years later was I able to say to him when he came out with his little ditties once again, that I was quite happy with my colour and did not choose to be white. How perfect my lies: I used to pray that as I grew my skin would stretch and it would go lighter! This lad also had a penchant for squirting ink from his fountain pen up the back of a young and really nice female Chemistry teacher, when we all got to the grammar school.

She was a nice lady and though I was not tempted to tell her who had done it, I often used to wonder what she would think when she took her lab coat off. In any event, she could not have been more pleasant or friendlier with all of us in her Chemistry group. She was a really kind soul and I would want to go to her today and thank her for being a good teacher and a nice person and say I am sorry that I did not feel able to tell her who squirted ink down her pale lemon lab coat.

At this time I was the only coloured person in the school. The same applied at senior school. A little later an Indian boy joined, but by this time things were a bit calmer. I used to find it would come in cycles. Some weeks would be fairly calm and others would be miserable. Sadly, I learned to spread some of the nasty words. I realised that one's colour was only one of the things that could be used to hurt. At first, if someone was mean to me I would simply walk away. Of course at school the option to hide is a limited one. Regrettably I soon found out, especially when cornered, that hitting back with hateful words of my own made their cruel words stop sooner and also made people more wary of repeating such things in the future. Having grasped this I then found things that set them apart. This was a particularly bad time as I realised I had become them. I was returning to them unacceptable behaviour that they gave me. You can see that this was the road to hell and if I had continued with it then everyone's existence at school would have been a miserable one, including my own. This is not something I wanted either for myself, or them, no matter if their words had hurt me. I needed school to propel me forwards into more learning, more training and a good job, if not a profession – not be a place of attrition where only the strongest came through.

Mercifully, I realised that hard work earned me respect. It also gave me a sense of worth. I am sure we can all see that constantly being shouted at with cruel and offensive words can destroy one's self esteem and I do accept that things could have turned out very differently for me. Thus, classroom success was like the lowest common denominator. I had to get through school and to do really well. This was the only path through for me.

I became a model pupil. Somehow, being called a 'swot' was the highest of compliments. Pupils would come to me to ask for help, if they were having trouble. I always completed and never missed a homework deadline. If I had difficulty I would find out how to do it. Once again hard work saved me and I became a better person, albeit someone who still thirsted after top marks. I was particularly good at Maths and had a mind that could at that time store rows of working in my head before writing down the answer. I also found, at grammar school, I had a keen interest in all the sciences especially Physics and Chemistry. Biology was less exciting but I did not find it difficult.

The other relevant point is that the teaching at the private school had put me, although I was a bit of a 'thicky' there, ahead of the whole class. There were only two girls in class who could beat me. One of the girls was good at maths, Hilary and one of them, Patsy, at English. They were very sharp and very quick. I spent all my time in a friendly pursuit to beat them. I remember one afternoon the headmaster set us a task of memorising a few lines of a poem and as soon as we could recite them to him, we could leave. It took me three goes. I think Hilary and Patsy did it straight off. The headmaster, Mr Sandham, crowed with delight and announced to the whole room, “At last, we have found something that he can’t do.” It didn’t last long. I went away and worked on any of my deficiencies that had come to light. It struck me however that although I didn’t have the smartest brain in class, by doing more work than anyone else I could still beat them. As you can see it took me a while to join the human race and retain a more balanced view. I am not sure I would have liked to have been in the same class as me in those days! In my defence my thirst to self-improve and to get better and better was, at that time, the fuel that moved me forwards. I was like a relentless machine geared solely in the pursuit of beating everyone else and gaining higher marks.

Please don’t think that Clarendon Road was a bad school. The staff and Mr Sandham were lovely kind people. Once things had settled I was very happy there and the fact that we did not get any homework was a great bonus. Today when my young patients come in with Clarendon Road uniforms on, I tell them what a super school it is and joke with mums and dads that some great people came out of that school!

Other things were noteworthy too. The boys and girls at private school were mostly from well to do homes and were always turned out in spotless uniforms and blazers. I remember with pride my new blazer and as I went down to the cloakrooms a little boy came up the steps and was promptly sick all over me and my new blazer! It was never quite the same again.

Things were very different at Clarendon Road even though nobody was ever sick on me! On my first day I noticed that the boy who sat next to me was very dirty, had worn clothes and was smelly. I went home and told my mum. She asked me how I felt about that. I told her that I soon got used to it, that he was a nice boy and that I had lent him my pencil sharpener. She smiled at me and said that was a good thing to have done.

I remember the day that it was one lad's birthday. He came to school and had not been given any presents by his mum or dad. His mum came to school at lunchtime when we were in the playground. She brought him his present and apologised that she'd not got him anything. She handed it over in a little brown paper bag, which was all creased. It wasn't wrapped up. He fished it out from the bag; it was a little Airfix model kit of a hovercraft. I told him that I thought it was a super present as I did not want him to feel bad. Inwardly, however, I could not help but think of the presents I received at home. There was one Christmas when things hit a low point when I was very little and my sister found a large plastic train in the wardrobe. She showed me and told me that it was a Christmas present. Our Mum was distraught by this and told her that I had nothing else for Christmas – but things improved from that time on. It brought it home to me that kids faced lots of other issues at home and looking a bit different was only one of the things that could separate people out. The boy whose mummy brought the present for him is still a local boy and has done very well for himself.

The final cruel truth came towards the end of my time at Clarendon Road. I had started to pick prizes up for good work. I found that Hilary and Patsy would vie with me and in Patsy's case this would continue in Eccles Grammar. I still have the books that I was given as prizes. "Prize for Good Work, 1968" which was 'A Book of Real Science' and "Prize for Science Work Books, 1969" which was 'First Days of the World'. I was in the library and the headmaster told me that I could look through the books on offer and decide which one I wanted as a 'prize'. I was alone when a senior boy came in. "I know what you are," he said triumphantly. I waited, for I knew that something dreadful was about to issue forth. I was not to be disappointed. "You're a half-caste!" he said. I had never heard this term in my life but I knew then and there that he was correct and that it also applied unequivocally to me. Something also told me that this was an even more specific descriptor than either 'coon' or 'wog' but was somehow even more offensive.

I said, "I'm not!"

"You are," he said, "I have seen your mum and dad collect you."

I moved quickly out of the little library and knew that this was my final explanation. The truth that everyone had known, but me. Although it is not used in polite society and is regarded as a term of abuse, I quite like it. It's what I am and I am proud of what I am and how it has forged me to be hard working, successful and more latterly at least – kind. I use it at every verse end and am very happy to be so described. Strangely, in my experience the most racist of people are the most offended by it.

At night, every night, while Dad was running his surgery we would sit in our lounge upstairs watching people come and go to the Blue Bell. Mum would do reading, writing and maths and Jane and I would lap it all up. She would also play records on the radiogram that nearly electrocuted me. 'Telstar' was the first record I remember and as you'll know it was one of these new 45's. Happy days!

When our girls were growing up, we would make sure that we read to them every night. They started bringing home word cards from school at the age of 3. As they got a little older they would then read to us. I remember when Emmie was eight she read night after night after night Secret Garden. This was the full version. I don't know how she got through it but she did reach the end. I remember too she had a wonderful pictorial encyclopaedia. We would go through this a few pages each night. It showed a drawing of a pregnant lady. I said, "Look there's the baby in a mum's tummy." Emmie then said to me, "Yes, Dad but how does the baby get in there?" I suggested that she ask her mum one night!

On one occasion when Emmie was about 5, we were parked near Barclays bank in Patricroft. On the wall were some obscene words. Emmie started assembling them. "F", "U", "C", she began. I said at this point, "Oh I just think I'll turn the car round as mum will be here in a minute!"

We had a vast number of books from school and ones that we'd bought. We didn't miss a night and the girls read some amazing stories. At Christmas we would change the theme and read magical Christmas stories. We were also fortunate in that at this time Harry Potter was very much in vogue – as always!

CHAPTER VI

Bacon

Being a devout Muslim, my Dad, of course, did not drink. I only ever saw him ever have one drink and that was the day my sister got married. He told us that he was happy to let us choose our own religion and as things were easier and less complicated we chose the Christian faith. At my sister's wedding, there was a toast to the bride and groom. Everyone raised a glass of champagne to them. My Dad raised his glass with some champagne in it and drank to them too. This was the only time I ever saw him drink. What was significant and what made my Dad, in my eyes, such a great man was the fact that *this* day and *this* toast was about them, their wishes and their beliefs and he chose to put, for that moment, his own beliefs to one side in order to honour theirs. I don't know many people who are so committed to their religion and would or could have still done that.

I would on occasion be in friends' houses when they were about to have their tea. I would often get asked to stay but would always make my excuses as I didn't want my Mum to worry where I was and so on. Often, however, the smell of bacon was tantalising. I had never tasted it. I asked my Mum if we could have bacon. She told me that this was not possible as Dad would not eat it. I told her that this was no problem, as he would not have to eat it. She smiled indulgently and said that this would not be the right thing either, as the smell would not be nice for him and he would not want to have food cooked later in the same pan. I understood, albeit with a little reluctance.

My friend, Robin, invited me to go away with him and his Mum and Dad in their caravan. This was a tow caravan and after an hour or two we were at the campsite. In those days there were the original TV dinners from Birds Eye that came on rectangular foil trays that were heated in the oven. My Mum had given me the beef one on several occasions. However, I knew that there was also a chicken one. The chicken offering had a pork sausage right in the middle. Mrs Wernick, Robin's Mum, pulled the TV dinners out of the oven and there on my lap was a chicken dinner; one complete with pork sausage. My mouth watered; here at last was my object of desire – a little pork sausage. I was not sure whether to eat it at once or save it until last, or even to eat half now and half at the end. Before I could come to a decision, Mr Wernick's fork flashed forward like a burst of lightning. He skewered my sausage with the words, "John, I am not sure your dad would like you eating that." He then popped this wonderful treat, my sausage, into his mouth and ate it! This is a fascinating vignette in that the Jewish chap would be so concerned about the Muslim chap's feelings in letting his son eat a pork sausage and was determined to 'protect' him from such influences.

This was typical of Mr Wernick, who though a devout Jew himself would always want to do right by others. I often think that if it had been left to Mr Wernick and my Dad they could have almost singlehandedly solved the problems of the Middle East! I remember at Mr Wernick's funeral, the Rabbi said that he was proud to be a local Jewish businessman and never sought to hide this fact from others. Alex Ferguson was at that funeral. I remember too in his garage he had a beautiful watercolour on the wall in his office. This watercolour is of Sir Matt Busby with his arms raised in the middle of a packed Old Trafford. In his writing it is signed, 'To my old friend, Hymie' (Mr Wernick). What an amazing original to have on your wall!

It won't surprise you to learn that my Dad was more than happy to entertain other people's faith. We would often go up to Prestwich on a Sunday morning and buy salami and bagels. The salami was, as you'll guess, Kosher. My Dad said he was quite happy with this and it was really the same as Halal. I remember my Mum saying that in the early days of their marriage they went to Rusholme where there was to be found a Halal butcher, itself pretty rare in those days. They wanted some chicken and the chap prepared to cut the poor thing's throat. My Mum ran out and I am not aware they ever went back!

He did not miss very much from South Africa; perhaps the sunshine and also perhaps the fresh fruit. He used to buy tinned Mango and tinned Guava. As you all know, these days fresh ones are on every supermarket shelf, but at that time they were pretty rare and he had to make do with the tinned variety. A couple of years ago, Frankie and I were on holiday in Cyprus and this lady at breakfast asked me what type of fruit I had put on my plate. I told her that it was fresh Guava and she told me that she had not seen it before. I told her that it was really tasty, much nicer than the tinned, but she should watch out for all the pips. Of particular delight was Mebos. There were different varieties of Mebos. Basically it is dried apricot (they do similar ones in Guava too) which is mixed with sugar and salt. Some is formed into little cakes, some cut into strips and tossed in sugar and the last kind which I have not seen since I was a little boy is rolled flat like parchment. The whole thing is dried. This last one was amazing and my sister and I would tear strips off the rolls of it and eat it. Without doubt childhood memories are powerful things, but I have not tasted anything like it since. Interestingly you can buy the cake-like Mebos on Amazon and it's not bad. Occasionally my sister or I send off for a batch of it and we share it out.

My Dad's relatives would send him two or three times a year a shipment of dried fruit, Mebos, Biltong and various nuts. He in turn would buy English biscuits in tins, parcel them up and ship them down to South Africa. I would wonder what state they would be in when they arrived there. I emailed a company in South Africa recently and asked if they could export some Mebos as supplies seem to have dried up on Amazon. They emailed back to say they could only supply it by the tonne. I was trying to work out if I could get through this amount before it went off or if, when I retire, I could open a little shop that sells it. Biltong is strips of dried meat like turkey and it is not only very salty but it is also very tough and only advised for those of you who have very strong teeth.

Around this time there was an interesting development on the telly. It was 1968 and I was still at Clarendon Road. Enoch Powell was giving his 'Rivers of Blood' speech, which has long since passed into English history. My Dad was sitting quietly watching. My Mum, however, was on her feet and screaming at the telly, almost shaking her fist with emotion.

"Yes, that's right, quite right, kick them out, kick all of them out. Quite right!"

My Dad, typically, sat there quietly but I remember my Mum was quite animated by this speech. This was the other little idiosyncrasy of our family, not only were our parents of very different and devout faiths but they also had polar opposite political views and Mum in particular was right-wing while Dad was more left-leaning, much though she tried to tell him that his views were much closer to hers than he realised!

Somehow, they held it together and although they lived quiet lives, guests would always remark how quiet and serene the house was. Indeed a friend from school remarked that he thought we could easily keep a wild animal in the house and everyone would be quite safe. The other point is that my Dad was a bit older than most of my friends' Dads. He would help me to build a kite, for instance, but I would do the running. This extended to most things and when I think of how much help we have given and how involved Frankie and I have been with our girls it seems especially strange. Having to sort things out myself however tended to make my mind more agile and me much more robust. I learnt from an early age to be self-reliant and the various insults I received along the way made me, at times, very tough and resilient. My Dad did not even come to my Graduation ceremony when I qualified in medicine. This does not mean that he wasn't proud of both my sister, and me but he was a quiet man who liked to stick to the background, although of course my Mum was there, Rodney and my sister-in-law.

Although my Dad was not especially sporty, I was lucky to have some super friends and neighbours. The Lennards on one side had two girls and a boy. The Deans the other way had three boys and the Fryers at the back had a boy and boy/girl twins. They were great people to play with and my Dad took cine footage of various school functions and parties we went to, before we left the house! The Deans and Lennards were related and each had businesses like department stores in Eccles and in Salford. I was often invited to accompany them on days out and the Deans took me to the Motor Show at Earls Court one year and the Fryers took me to an Army fun day where we got to look at armoured cars and fire (fixed!) machine guns. In any event, we had a great childhood and were always playing out. Even at night time we would still be playing out round Worsley golf course.

When I was very little, Monton railway station had been closed but some of the track and many of the signals were still in place. Two friends and I had climbed to the top of this really tall signal right where the old Monton station used to be. Today this would not be far from Monton Medical Centre. We were hanging on really high up and the signal was swaying in the breeze. We looked over the fields towards Parrin lane. Several cars had stopped and a motorist had stopped a policeman. They were all pointing to us at the top of the signal. The policeman started to come across the fields that were there then and we thought we'd better beat a hasty retreat. We rushed down the signal and then ran for home. I told my friends to change the colour of their jumpers and maybe we would not be recognised and we could continue to play outside. Within a week or two all the signals were removed and the remains of the track torn up. I often think of the old station in Monton and also Worsley as we go for walks along this route. I recently read a book that one of my patients lent me and it had some detailed pictures of Worsley station and how magnificent it was. I see there is a lot of debate about the new guided busway. I can't help but think of that wonderful train that ran right through and maybe could have tempted a few drivers who clog up the roads.

It was also the time of the National Front. They were quite active on the news and on the telly at that time and they were insisting that foreigners would be repatriated as soon as they'd gained power. This made me very nervous, as I was not sure as a young lad what would happen. I read just this week in the paper about the Labour party being engulfed in the anti-semitism row. One correspondent wrote that he would visit his Jewish granny who would keep a packed suitcase, 'just in case there was trouble'. In my younger days I grew up with very similar fears that something dreadful would happen to us. In fact, I think most of my young life was spent in the shadow of fear. Would they simply repatriate my Dad, leaving our Mum in England, or him and us two kids, or all of us for having the temerity to cross racial divides? Mercifully, I never did find out, but I was very worried and my only answer, without doubt, was to keep studying and to make sure that I was the best I could possibly be. It seems that my childhood ended at the age of six, but it was a trade that I could not reverse.

One day my sister came running in. She'd been on the bus to Manchester. The conductor, who was a Pakistani gentleman screamed at the top of his voice as she'd got on. "Well, well, what have we here. Where are you from then?" Most English folk would never have behaved in this way, but I remember she was very upset and found such comment hard to take. It is my experience that the English are much more accepting and a lot less controversial, but of course it's hard to make sweeping conclusions.

I remember too the long walks we'd have in Worsley village. My cousin had a very tiny stone-built cottage on Leigh Road. This was near the 'monument' at the back and one could walk out of his back garden to the monument, which I am told is still there but in a poor state these days. His little house, too, has long since been pulled down and nowadays the whole road contains only massive mansions. It's a shame his little stone cottage with the club-shaped windows and beautiful carved-wood gable end barge-boards is not still there. On a Sunday we'd walk from his house down to the Worsley Courthouse and buy ice-cream. As you'll have guessed, in those days there was no motorway and it's perhaps a good thing that so many more-recent residents cannot remember the time before they built it as Worsley was truly beautiful. In a similar vein, I remember walking through Worsley Woods and this was a magical place but much was changed when they drove the motorway, with its high-rise concrete elevated sections, right through the middle of it. I do remember them building the motorway as my friends and I would go cycling on there and the workmen would chase us away.

We would also cycle through Trafford Park on a Sunday and how this has changed since then. One of my favourite treks, however, was when we'd heard about the Black Harry Tunnel, which we learned had collapsed some years before. We cycled from Monton under the Quaker's bridge and onwards. It was during a summer holiday and each day we would go a bit further. By the end of the holiday we'd got to the far side of the East Lancs and found the old route of the Black Harry tunnel. In truth there wasn't much to see but in common with most 'adventures' it was the journey not the arriving that was most exciting!

Chapter VII

Sabre

Disaster struck the summer of 1969. One day we came in to school and we were told that we were going to sit the 11-Plus that day. We sat down and did the test and didn't think too much about it. Many of my friends passed to go to Eccles Grammar. One of my close friends who was very clever and had easily earned his place, was told by his father that he wasn't to go to Grammar school as he was expected to join the family tyre business as soon as he was able. He did go into the family business but soon after went into a completely different line of work and became very successful. Unsurprisingly, a place at Grammar school was not wanted by everyone, and indeed so many went on to do other things, that they achieved great success in, that did not require more advanced education.

One of the teachers suggested to my parents that I sit the exams for Bolton School and also Manchester Grammar. Mr Sandham, the headmaster, said that Eccles Grammar had been a perfect choice for his son and it would be for me too. My parents took his advice. I was delighted to be going as Eccles Grammar was just up the road. They said I could pop home for lunch rather than have school dinners, as long as I was back in time for afternoon classes.

I settled down to a long summer school holiday and looked forward to starting. In those days the first three years wore green blazers and in fourth and fifth years you could wear a black blazer and then in 6th form you could wear your own clothes.

The Deans next door had a wonderful aluminium beer barrel in their outside shed. In a move reminiscent of the circus acts, I started to walk on this and found that it was quite easy to go back and forth. The edges were also bevelled and, by putting pressure on one side or the other, one could get the barrel to turn. I became quite adept at this and also quite confident. One of the boys told me that I was going to fall and then pushed me in the small of my back. I fell backwards and straight on to my right arm which then crumpled underneath me. He took me round to my Dad who was running his surgery. I must have been screaming the place down as it was really hurting and I tried to support it with my good arm. I could tell that it was broken as it was running at a very funny angle. My Dad was not someone who was quick to anger. He just said to the boy "What a naughty boy you are." That was about it. My Mum took me to Hope Hospital, which in those days had a Paediatric department, which I remember was on H1. I was admitted.

The registrar took my mum to one side and told her that my arm was badly broken. The wrist fracture was easy enough to sort but the elbow was badly shattered and the blood supply to the bones had been endangered. There were several fragments, which put my arm at risk as it was unlikely they would ever heal. He was not sure he could save it and he warned her that they might have to amputate.

I often wonder how my life would have turned out if I had in fact lost my right arm that day. I was kept in and a bed found for me on the children's ward.

At that point, I was not told any of this but I soon realised just how serious a plight I was in the middle of. A call was put out to Mr Green who was the senior Orthopaedic Surgeon. He was on holiday and was about to board the boat train at Southampton. He returned to Manchester that very night in order to save my arm. I didn't know this at the time and my Mum told me years later. I was kept in hospital for 2 weeks but not even this revealed how serious things were for me. As you'll know for most breaks, even ones that need plates in them, you are discharged within a day or so. Often if it just needs a plaster you are home within an hour or two. Even if it needs a quick anaesthetic to straighten a deformity, you are often discharged late the same day or the next. Not this one! There were various pins sticking out of it, which had been used to stabilise the fragments. Even this gave me no clue as to how bad things were for me. The thing that informed me just how much trouble I was in was something else entirely. My Dad appeared by my bed and asked me if he could get me anything. My Dad never went anywhere, and yet here he was. This was proof that I was in deep danger and my Dad's concerned expression reflected this. The very fact that he'd turned up meant something unusual and also something critical.

I could tell that he was very worried and very upset. I suspect that it was still a bit 'touch and go' for my arm. I asked him if I could have an Alsatian! I'd always loved these dogs and admired their intelligence, their devotion, loyalty and good looks! I am not sure if I was just pushing my luck as I did not expect my Dad to agree, or if I sensed how much danger I was in and thought this was a really useful counterweight to my predicament. I am not sure if it was his religion, but he was of the view that cats were much cleaner than dogs. When my sister and I were young he had a black cat called Peter, which was actually a female cat. Peter had died some years before. Although I don't think he was too keen on having a dog in the house, he barely hesitated and then agreed. I think this fact alone would have confirmed my worst fears about my condition. As soon as I came home after my two-week stay, we started looking for Alsatians. We found a lovely Alsatian puppy from a local breeder in Ellesmere Park. Dad suggested that we call the dog 'Sabre'. He also suggested that Sabre sleep in the garage and we made a bed for him in there. He howled so much that first night that we had to go and get him. Then my Dad suggested that he stay in the kitchen and a week or two later it was anywhere downstairs and eventually he had the run of the house.

Sabre was a wonderful dog and Dad became very fond of him, as people do, without doubt. The only sticky time was when my Dad's prayer times must have been close together. I remember he had this special calendar which dealt with sunrise and sunset and I think, though I am by no means certain, that prayer times varied with such events. Anyway he left his prayer mat out, and there on the prayer mat was the little hat he wore when he prayed and also he had some amber beads. Sabre strayed on to the prayer mat, which was like a little hearthside rug. When I was very young I wondered if it was a magic carpet. Anyway, my Dad was not one to raise his voice but he shouted at Sabre. I must confess I have never seen an Alsatian shift quite so quickly. Sabre came rushing downstairs and immediately ran behind the sofa. I think the dog had got used to my Dad's usually quiet nature and was shocked when he was being shouted at.

If my sister or I were naughty, he would threaten to take off his belt though he never rose to this. He had a more effective punishment for us, which would bring us into line without his having to lift a finger. He would simply announce "Mum, we'll have to send them to boarding school." This would produce wails of contrition from both my sister and me and was usually the most effective way of getting us back in line. Mum would always say that she had to be the tough one and she would fight the battles that my Dad was not keen on taking on. I understand this as I think, too, where possible one has to live in the sunlit uplands of one's life – where possible, though I accept it is not always possible to do such a thing.

Anyway, I digress. Sabre was a wonderful dog. He had lots of energy, put up with my merciless teasing and was always ready for a walk or a ride in the car. In fact if I was washing the car, he would sit there happily all afternoon. He was, without doubt, most excited when being conveyed and we would open the back window for him, just a bit, and he would stick his nose through to let the cold air waft over it. People would often stop and ask me if he was dangerous, but the truth of it was that he was as a very gentle dog. Other children would stop and ask me if he was a wolf when we were out walking. If we were feeding him and we'd forgotten to add the biscuits or something like that, then we'd simply pick his bowl up off the floor and he would sit and wait patiently, whimpering a bit, until we'd finished and his bowl was replaced. I don't know of many hungry big dogs that one could attempt this with but with him one never felt that he would bite. He was a long-haired Alsatian and would require lots and lots of brushing which my sister and I used to do several times a week. He would sit there quite happily as we brushed him for what seemed to take an age.

He was also amazingly intelligent and would recognise lots of words. We taught him to open the back door by pulling on a rope tied through the handle. If he came in from the garden, we would shout "Close", and without delay he would go back and push his body against the door until it closed. He was quite a hungry dog and my Dad would often say that cats know when they have eaten enough but dogs never do. Sometimes if we were having our tea and he had not had his meal yet – we used to feed him first but sometimes when the clocks changed, for a few days his normal patterns would be out of kilter – he'd sit at the table and give us his paw until we gave him something. If we then showed him our empty palms he would sigh a little and then go away. One day the clocks had changed and he was hungry. He came up to me and gave me his paw. I sent him away only for him to return a few minutes later. I then put my palms up and said "Gone", a signal that there was no food for him. The poor soul must have been teased terribly, so it's a good job he was good-natured and forgiving. At this he moved away quickly, but I saw that rather than sit in his usual spot he went into the kitchen. After a minute or two he returned. In those days my Mum had a typical Formica kitchen with the sliding doors. These were often left open and in one of these she kept all her tinned things. Sabre returned after a few minutes and I saw that he had a tin in his mouth. He came up to me and dropped the tin on my lap. Out of all the tins in the cupboard he'd chosen the one containing the dog food. He sat there patiently while I looked at this tin. Without any further prompting I went into the kitchen and fed him.

Sabre's hunger got him in trouble once or twice. Mrs Barber the lady next door but one had a guest-house. She used to come round with lots of uneaten food and was mystified as to why her guests would not eat it. She would give it to Sabre who would eat it all up. Within minutes the poor soul would rush out into the garden where he would spend the next half hour vomiting uncontrollably. This happened on two occasions. She used to call his name as she came round. On the third occasion as soon as he heard his name being called he ran and hid behind the sofa. We then waited for Mrs Barber to go before I buried it all in the garden. I had a feeling that poor Sabre had discovered what her guests already knew!

For such a fierce looking dog, as I said, Sabre was as soft as butter. One day on our way to North Wales we stopped for a picnic in Penmaenmawr and walked up this little hill. Sabre came with me and Jane. A sheep darted out of the hedge and Sabre ran all the way down the hill and jumped in the back of the car and refused to come out. In a way this was perfect because having a soft dog suited us but of course he looked the part and people did not mess with us. I would usually walk him four times a day and often I'd be walking through the golf course late at night. One night some really rough looking lads started to run towards me. Sabre had wandered on to the golf course. Feeling a bit frightened I called to him and he darted back through the little fence just as the lads were closing on me. I heard one of them say "Oh well, we won't bother then." To this day I wonder what would have happened to me had Sabre not been with me.

My lucky streak, of things going right just at the point of disaster, continued. It was about to extend to the dog. As a surly and less than co-operative teenager I got in the back of my Dad's car one day. In those days nobody wore seatbelts in the back. On that day, as usual, Sabre jumped in the back of the car with Jane and me. He would usually sit between us but if he started getting hot he would prefer to sit by the window with its cool glass. I remember that I had not closed the rear door properly, but was too lazy or fed-up to do so. My Dad was driving round Anglesey. Suddenly he turned off the road in a sharp left turn. As he did so Sabre slumped against the passenger door. His back paws were on the seat but his spine banged against the rear door lifting his front paws off the seat as he fell backwards against the door. In the next moment, the door opened. Sabre's back paws remained on the seat but he was now falling backwards through the open rear door. My sister looked towards the door just as I did. It was like one of these action films where the scene is played out in slow motion. What was really unsettling was the look of shock and utter betrayal on the poor dog's face. I don't know how I managed to move so quickly.

Frankly, if someone was telling me what happened next, I simply would not believe them. Anyway, as he continued to fall his two front paws came up off the back seat and he started tilting backwards. The thing that saved him, and me, was that his two paws remained close together. I somehow grabbed both together with my right hand and pulled him towards me and back into the car. The dog fell forwards but behind me as I leaned forwards. With my left hand I pulled on the door in order to close it. It must have taken place in less than a second. There was a car coming to the junction we were turning into. As we continued round the corner, my Dad sensed there was something wrong. He'd heard the sound of the rear door banging shut. He asked me what the noise was. I said, "Oh, it's nothing, Dad." We continued our journey and I will never know who was more relieved, me or the dog! I can only think, too, if he'd have fallen from the car through the back door at that junction he'd have been badly hurt or killed. Not a good way to treat your best pal and I learned that day, even if I was in a bad mood, to at least make sure that I'd properly closed the rear door.

Coming back to my right arm, I shudder when I see people driving along with their right arm dangling from the driver's window. It just goes through me. Then, you may have seen, the film 'Hot Tub Time Machine' where they go through gruesome scenarios as to how the poor bell-boy had lost his arm when they go back in time. A very funny but very rude film!

CHAPTER VIII

Eccles Grammar

The summer I broke my arm was the year we moved from Clarendon Road to Eccles Grammar. Mr Sandham had advised my parents that it would be a perfectly adequate school for me and he was correct. My arm remained in a sling for much of that summer. My Dad took some cine footage of Jane and me and my friend Robin running on Monton Green with Sabre as a puppy. In the pictures I still have the triangular sling. As the sling was on my right arm, I was encouraged to use my left hand. This was the arm I had favoured when I started out but my teachers had other ideas. I suppose in truth if I had been left handed I would have used this one to attempt to break my fall so perhaps the same thing would have happened but on the left!

Sabre, at that time a puppy, had that soft downy fur, the floppy ears and the big paws denoting the big dog he would slowly grow to become.

I also had to go back into hospital to have the two pins removed from my elbow. Mr Green warned me that I might not get my full range of movement back and he was correct; it also runs at a funny angle and clunks a little when I am in the gym. I never put too much weight on it and use the gym for keeping fit, tending to concentrate on my legs, and each movement that I do make with my right arm is a constant delight. The surgeon told me that my wrist had also been broken but he was not unduly worried as he thought it would heal much more quickly than my elbow. He did warn me that as I got older I would most likely have arthritis in my wrist and it is strange that this year and just recently it has started hurting more than ever. It's funny, the year I retire it starts to hurt. Some days it hurts even to write, so if any of you come in and see me rubbing my wrist you will know why.

I knew that I was never going to be able to dig roads. Being so small and having a dodgy right arm meant that this would have been unwise. Fortunately for me, and for so many others, Eccles Grammar was just about perfect. So much hot air is written about Grammar schools, how children are selected at the age of eleven and can be made to feel inferior, rejected and thrown to one side. I cannot really comment about this. There is so much political charge around this that it's difficult to see the light for the smoke. Also the politicians who scream the loudest about 'selecting children' are the ones who either went to very expensive public schools or private schools and they invariably send their own kids to such schools. I suppose I would want for my kids what they wanted for theirs and cannot apologise for it. Clever kids who come from poor homes should be given the chance at the very best education the country can provide and this should be paid for by the state.

Please feel free to shout at me if I am about to write a lot of bunkum but Eccles Grammar was a perfect vehicle for my plans. It gave me the tools to raise myself into a challenging and good job with good prospects as it did and also so many children like me – and it did not cost our parents a penny. So many came out of Eccles Grammar and went on to become doctors, dentists, accountants, lawyers, engineers and so on ad infinitum. I worry mostly today about the poor kids. Those kids who are from poor but good homes who happen to be really bright. I must confess that in any IQ test I have ever taken I only came out as being a little above average. I went to Eccles Grammar with some really bright kids. I burned, however, with the desire to do well to constantly better myself and my performance and beat in class as many as I could. No, I don't think I would have liked to have been in my class either! What drove me and continued to drive me were the events of when I was 6. I wondered what would happen to me if I could not get a good job or even any job, and this continued to burn within me at every verse end.

Anyway, what happens to the really poor kids from poor homes who happen to be bright? I think with a good, decent, free education as provided by a grammar school they will go on as so many of my peers did to become the brain surgeon or the rocket scientist or the guy (or girl!) who invents the next jet engine. I cannot see the Chinese or the Americans agonising over schools in this way, but there we are. Shout at me if you wish, but I think every boy or girl should have the chance of a free education to the same standard as the one I received. I cannot comment about these new fancy academies as I have never been to one but if they are not stretching our brightest boy or girl from any home then I'm sorry but they won't get the education I and so many others got. We owe our teachers everything. I sometimes bump into my old Biology teacher in Monton.

She keeps asking me not to call her Mrs Price and to call her Hilary. She has missed the point. It's a mark of my respect and, yes, my thanks for her and all my other teachers and the debt that I owe them. I want other kids to have the same chance that I had.

I wish politicians could sense that debt but of course they, as all rich people do, send their kids to good fee-paying schools and this is where the real inequality lays – the private school that can outpace the bog-standard state school. I'd better leave it there before you all put my windows in.

We had so many wonderful lessons from so many gifted teachers. I tended to gravitate towards the sciences, especially maths and physics. My form teacher, however, wrote on my report one year that to neglect the arts and languages would be a short-sighted approach and I therefore did my best to up my game. At the same time my French teacher told me that my performance was slipping and although I was in the top set for French she thought I was going to have to drop down into the lower set. I was determined not to let this happen. I went home each night and learnt ten new French words, conjugated the new verbs, revised ten old ones from the night before and ten random ones. I wrote them all down in a little exercise book. It did the trick; my performance started to improve and they did not ask me to drop down a set after this.

By and large, my time at Eccles Grammar was a very happy one. The summer I was due to start there my Mum bumped into a lady in Eccles who, I think, knew my Mum and Dad but not me or Jane especially well. She was telling my Mum that her son had failed his Eleven Plus but was not especially disappointed as he was looking forward to going to school with me. I did not know this boy. My Mum apologised and told her that she was sorry but I had passed for the Grammar school and would be starting there come September.

The other major plus was that the school was only one-hundred yards away and the headmaster said that if I got back in time for afternoon classes, I could go home for lunch. This was great because it meant that I could manage to shovel my lunch down quickly and also walk the dog. My Mum used to say to Sabre, "John, will be coming in from school." And he would go and watch through the window. The same would happen at home time and I would take him out for another walk then. Then I'd do my homework, have my tea and, for a final time, take him out again before I went to bed. I think as part of the deal about having an Alsatian my Dad said I would have to look after him and I was keen not to disappoint – apart from, if one forgets, nearly throwing him through the rear car door! Both Jane and I would also spend a long time brushing him as he had a long coat.

The downside to being allowed home for lunch was a big one. In my first year I would walk down the road to our house on Monton Green. I would invariably see two boys coming the other way who I think must have been from Monton Unitarian school which, a bit like Eccles Grammar, has been closed down, though not pulled down, a long time ago. These two boys would set about me as soon as they saw me. Their typical greeting was as follows. "You look like Sambo. Where are you going Sambo? Is your name Sambo because you look like Sambo?" Sometimes they would throw stones or sticks at me and I would scurry away.

This went on for all of that first year. I knew that this was something I had to deal with and at first I would just do my best to run past them. I hadn't yet developed my thick skin and they could tell that they were hurting which, without doubt, only adds to the bully's delight. As things do, however, the story turned a little more. There were two lads. One was a fat lad and the other had sticky-out ears. Of course people in glass houses and so on. The following year I once again started at Eccles Grammar, only now I felt a little more senior – I was in year 2 and all the freshers started. I was still in a green blazer. In the first couple of weeks of the new academic year, I was hanging my coat up in the cloakroom. There also hanging his coat was the fat lad. We were otherwise alone. My anger rose like boiling mercury. I went over to him and said "Where are you going Fatso. Is your name Fatso cos you look like Fatso?" Mercifully my anger was discharged by somehow finding the strength for me to bodily pick him up and hang the back of his blazer on one of the coat hooks – with him still in it! I was so exhausted by this and it was a good thing or I think I would have started laying into him. I left him hanging by his blazer from one of the pegs. I screamed at him, "Not so tough now, eh, Fatso? Where is your friend with the monkey ears?"

That was the thing; if I'd had the strength I would have happily really hurt him. I'm not proud of this and, of course, apart from a few things like sticks and the odd stone they threw at me they never assaulted me. Through the lens of a twelve year old, however, it felt strangely satisfying. Here it was, however, monkey-eared friend had not got into the Grammar school. My message was very clear – to work harder and harder and this would separate me from those who were keen to show their distaste and dislike of me. Of course the vast majority of kids, especially at the Grammar school, were really nice kids. They were not in any way affected or put off by my unusual appearance or indeed, once again, of my being the only coloured lad in school.

Some years later I was walking round Lymm with a girl friend. It was a lovely Sunday afternoon and we were quietly walking along. A lad on a bicycle came riding on the pavement and nearly bumped into me. I was just about to apologise, as one does. He had a very different scenario in mind. He shouted a the top of his voice, "Out of my way you fu**in coon. Fu**in wog!" I must confess that I raced after him. He cycled off and I would like to be able to tell you that he had to get a move on. This can only be seen as a good thing as if I had caught him, I would have surely killed him. Such incidents would cause my anger to spiral out of control and it was not always possible to channel it into more productive ways. In truth I only learned this much later in life.

Three of my patients, all young men, destroyed their lives in moments of uncontrolled anger. I suspect I could have easily done this on more than one occasion. One of them came in with his arm in plaster. I asked him what he'd been up to and he told me that he'd lost his temper while driving. Another driver had cut him up on the road and he'd followed him and eventually caught up with him. He had then gone over to the other driver, still sitting in his car and banged on the windscreen with such force that he'd broken his wrist. I then asked him a chilling question. "Were you at work when this happened?" He hung his head and then told me that it was true the event took place when he'd been working. If I tell you that he was a petrol tanker driver on

£80,000 a year, you will get some idea of the horror of this episode and how it must have played being pursued by an angry driver in a petrol tanker! Poor chap has not worked since and it is now many years ago.

Having matured considerably over the years, my anger tends to only come out when I am driving. I used to have a wonderful sports car, a Mazda Rx8 which was capable of truly scary speeds and when doing so would purr along like a turbine as it had a Wankel engine. One day we were driving north on the M6 and this chap really cut me up. I chased after him for some distance but eventually calmed down. Some miles later a similar thing happened but mercifully I managed to control myself much better. Unbeknown to me, one of my patients was witnessing this second incident. He came in to see me a week later. He told me that he'd said to his wife, "Look there's Dr Behardien and that chap has really cut him up and he didn't react at all." I was suitably humbled by this incident and a short time later sold the car and bought a bright green Mazda 2 which had a very small engine and pedestrian performance! It was also much more frugal with petrol as the Rx8 could only manage about 17 miles to the gallon!

While out walking my dog one day; we were walking along the path through Worsley Golf course. Sabre liked to dart under the fence and he would often walk through the long grass. This was especially the case if another dog was coming the other way and he would prefer to avoid contact with other dogs. A fairly stout lady in a tweed two-piece suit was coming towards me. She had a long walking stick, which she brandished with relish. There were only two of us. As she approached but still some way off she shouted "N-word" and then once again at the top of her voice. In those days the N-word was sometimes used and I appreciate these days it is deeply offensive. I wondered who she could possibly be talking to. I must confess I turned round to see if anyone was behind me. At this point the path splits into a fork. I took the right fork as she came down the left fork. As the lady came closer, once again she shouted "N-word!". I was very puzzled as she didn't know me and I couldn't think I had upset her in some way! I then turned left at the top of the golf course and left again to come down the left fork, the one that the lady had come down. She must have turned back as once again she was approaching. Once again she shouted the N-word. Once again there was only the two of us. She now passed me and smiled and said "Good morning!" I mumbled something similar back to her. As soon as she passed me she shouted, "N-word!". I turned round just in time to see this magnificent black Labrador appear coming under the fence from the golf course, just as my own dog did some minutes' later.

I know that Guy Gibson, who led the Dambuster missions, also had a black dog called 'N-word'. I am sure in its day people didn't think twice about naming their dogs in this way. It seems things move on. For some time I would see this lady and she would always be very friendly towards me and I would usually see her with her black Labrador, called N-word!

Doing well in class was my constant defence and I was always keen to come top. One or two of us did so well that they created a new prize at speech day for 'Attainment'. I got one of these prizes and so did my friend Patsy from Clarendon road. The other really clever girl from Clarendon road also went to the Grammar school but she seemed to lose that 'hunger' that continued to burn inside me. At

Clarendon road I had come top in maths with 96%. The teacher sat down next to me and told me that some of my classmates had only got 32%. She showed me a graph with the spread of marks from top to bottom. On this she then drew another line and from this she re-read all the marks. She told me that this would mean that I had now got 80% but the chap at the bottom would have 45%. She asked me if this was acceptable to me. I asked her if it meant I had still come top. She smiled and promised me that this would not change. I agreed.

I was especially good at Physics and really enjoyed the lessons. At Eccles Grammar, we had a super teacher. One day he set us some homework. It seemed easy to me and though it was not due for a few days I rattled it off that night. My 'friend' came to me the following day. He said he was having trouble with it and could I help him. Perhaps if I could let him borrow my Physics homework book it would be clear. I told him that he could borrow my book with pleasure and thought no more about it. A few days later we had another Physics lesson. The teacher gave out the books, having now marked our homework, but before he did so he told us the tale of the two monkeys on the moon each with a typewriter. He went on, "it's said that if we wait long enough and given them enough paper then these two monkeys will eventually bash out every word that has ever been written by man." He then gave out the books and said that my account was identical to my friend's. What I did not realise was that my 'friend' had copied my work word for word and then very cleverly added a couple of lines on the bottom. This then looked as if I had copied from him. I explained to the teacher what had happened and looked at my friend and asked him to confirm that this was the case.

He giggled a little and said some unintelligible words but refused to confirm that he'd simply copied my work. I was really upset as the teacher obviously did not believe me. He was suspicious of me from that day forwards. I don't think he ever believed that mine was the original account. Nor did my colleague ever admit it or even try to come to my assistance. I thought he was a super teacher, one that I really admired. Unfortunately from that day onwards I just had to prove that I was so good at Physics that I did not need to copy someone else's work in order to do well. Once again burning within me was the need to outpace all others. The other thing that it taught me was that some friends were no such thing. Some years later this lad got married. It was one of these massive, massive weddings: there must have been 300 guests. I don't think we've spoken since.

We took one 'O' level a year early. This was English Language. We were in the Black Blazers by this time. I could only manage a grade 2. English language was not my strong suit and this is why I decided to revisit it with my writing some years later. We had a really nice young teacher, who insisted on sitting on the desk right at the front of the class, sporting a really short skirt. It is perhaps one reason why the boys did not do as well as the girls!

The following year I'd got things well sorted. All the O-levels I took I attained grade 1. It had never been done before at Eccles Grammar. By this time politicians had 'done for' the Grammar school. We were the last form through to receive a Grammar school education. A few years later the school was pulled down. Those who wanted to do 'A' levels went on to Eccles Sixth Form college. Most of the Grammar teachers moved to Eccles College and our super education was renewed.

I was very keen to do Electronics by this time and at home I would build little circuits. A lot of the components would have slim coloured bands on them which would denote their value. I'd also started my Ham Radio exams at night school and passed these a short time later. Sadly, I could not afford the equipment and though I got my Amateur radio licence I never actually got on the air. One could always use CB for Citizen Band but it was never as fully featured or as powerful as Ham Radio as by using more useful frequencies one could do long distance and bounce the signal over to Australia and other delights that I can just about remember. I suppose, too, that I was one of a group of original nerds. While others spoke of football we would be drawing circuit diagrams of amplifiers and DX (Distance) Transmitters. Valves were the order of the day because solid state devices like transistors, that are the building blocks of modern 'chips', were still in their infancy and most importantly were either very expensive or could not handle the power of valves, or both! I went to a careers convention and was speaking to one of the lecturers there. I had found out by this time that I had a red/green colour deficiency and told the lecturer. I was absolutely brimming with enthusiasm about a career in Electronics but without any preamble he simple told me to, "Forget it!" I was obviously going to have to come up with something else! In my room you will see charts that we use to test for colour blindness and deficiencies. The one that reads to most people '18' is not what I see but a '13'. Red-green deficiencies are the most common.

We all turned 17 at Eccles College and many of us were keen to learn to drive. Once we'd done this we would then borrow a parent's car and on one or two days a week drive to college. Eccles College even had a little car park for such students just outside the gate. The usual form would be to drive through the gate and then use the full width of the teachers' car park to turn, then come out again and finally park in the students' car park.

My friend Stella did this one morning. It had been raining. She'd borrowed her mum's car and through the gate she went. She began to turn as soon as she entered the staff car park and then began to brake. Her foot slipped off the brake and on to the accelerator. She continued to accelerate just as the car was turning. In turn she banged into one, two, three, four, five, six teachers' cars. The poor soul, I saw her afterwards and she told me what had happened. She told me that she just felt sick. Of course the teachers were none too pleased but fortunately no one was hurt. There was then a new rule, quickly introduced, that students were not allowed to drive through the gates and certainly not into the staff car park. I am sure this event weighed heavily on not only poor Stella's insurance, but also her mum's too for some years to come. I suspect that if a 17-year old did that today the unfortunate person would not be able to drive, or to afford to drive, for many years to come.

As we'd come up through the grammar school and moved to Eccles College most of us had matured significantly. There was very little teasing and very little bullying. As I hope I have made clear most kids were unaffected by one's colour or indeed many of the other things that one can be teased with. One lad, however, had either not matured enough or could not leave such things alone. He had a friend who joined him in his efforts of making fellow students' lives a misery. I remembered this friend of his; he was weeping in the changing rooms when we first started at Eccles Grammar. Because of my arm injury, the surgeon suggested that I should not do sports until the New Year at the earliest. I thought this was a sensible precaution and was happy to do the boot cleaning. The other lad was not allowed to do sports for reasons that escape me but I remember when he started weeping I took the view that it wasn't going to help, but he seemed like a nice lad. His friend, however, was a very different sort and took him the complete wrong way. The thuggish boy was a very big lad and of course widely known as a Judo black belt. Very few went up against him and the few that did were crushed in the full sense of that word. I remember he drove a GT6, which was the sporty-backed version of the Triumph Spitfire. It must have cost a fortune to insure – but I expect to his parents nothing would have been too expensive for their little darling – who was a nasty type.

I remember things came to a particularly cruel head on the A-level Biology trip to Lledr Hall. This was my second such trip. By this time there were one or two other coloured lads in the school. We'd all got on the coach and of course the nasty lad was sitting at the back with his entourage. As everyone assumed their seats he started calling from the back. One of the Asian lads was about to sit down and the bully shouted from the back as if he were loading the coach. "Oh, here's another spade!" I had never heard this term used other than for a digging implement. This is the thing about cruel words; their meaning translates instantly by the vehemence and context in which they are used. I assumed that the word 'spade' is used for a black person or a coloured person and I assumed also that it is a derogatory term. Of course he wasn't finished and as I sat down, he shouted, "Oh here's a half caste!" Only that was the thing; it had lost its double meaning and although he and his entourage started giggling hysterically it had ceased to have an insulting or derogatory context for me. All the insults had been delivered and I was starting to feel much happier in my skin. This is why I often describe myself as a half-caste mainly because I am proud of my journey and what it's made me.

Of course he wasn't finished there and, mercifully, I was not in his dormitory. I remember they were looking for the local Spar as they were hoping to buy beer. Only as the coach drew away did they spy it and I having been before knew exactly where it was. One lad in their dorm was not part of their clique and he had an especially bad time. They started calling him 'scum' and for a while it got quite nasty.

My learning by this time was a well-oiled machine. My mathematics was really good and my young brain was also good at assembling lines of problems in my head and then just writing down the answer. My Maths teacher, like all that had come before, advised against this because if I got the answer wrong then I would not get any marks as I could not demonstrate the working. He asked me to explain how I'd arrived at an answer one day and I went through it. He told me that he would not have done it that way but the correct answer had been arrived at. One of the girls, Gwyneth, in my maths set laid into me one day – not in an unfriendly way. "You think you are really good at maths but I think it's just a load of hot air." Half an hour later I was sitting doing nothing. The teacher had set us some work. He asked me if I had finished. He then said that if I had finished I shouldn't just sit there; I might as well start the homework that he'd set.

"I have finished that as well, Sir." Yes, yes, I know, I wouldn't like to be at school with me either!

"Oh in that case, John, you can go."

I packed my things up and as I passed Gwyneth's desk I gave her a little wink.

The bullying lad went on to be a drug rep. Some years later when I was a GP in Eccles one of his colleagues came in and said that he was now a manager and was high up in the organisation. I was hoping to meet up with him as I would have wished to ask him which were his products. I would then have told him calmly that I would never by choice use any of them and would always strive to use competitors'. Mercifully I never did meet up with him and had the presence of mind not to ask his colleague which products he was responsible for. I cannot promise to be a perfect person but I learned as I went along and realised fairly early on that harbouring dark thoughts about others damaged me and diminished me at the same time. I would have loved to follow GT-6 home. Although we were all aged 17/18, the seeds of his antipathy for his fellow men must surely have been gifted to him by his parents.

When we left the small private school my friend Robin went to Stand Grammar. Of course we'd all had a sheltered life (in some ways!) at the small school and many of us had rude awakenings. Robin tells me that he was set upon on his first day at school. The boy in question went home that evening and told his dad that, he'd beaten up a 'filthy Jew'. His Dad gave him a good hiding and instructed him to apologise the following day, which he did. Robin tells me that he and the boy eventually became good friends. I suspect that households like these were and are more in the majority but of course there are to this day households where very different views are expounded.

The other thing is that the best friend of our GT-6 driver, the one who was sobbing in the changing rooms because he couldn't do sports, used to tell everyone he was going to do dentistry at University. Sadly, no, he didn't make it. I suspect if he'd put a little more work into his studies and a little less into emulating his thuggish friend, things would have gone better for him.

My Maths tutor suggested to my Mum and Dad that I apply to Oxford. I must have been mad because really all I ever wanted was to go to a local University. I had been advised against electronics because of my colour deficiency and had decided against mechanical engineering and also architecture. Almost by exclusion I ended up choosing Medicine and applied to Oxford. My Dad told me that if I went to Manchester and stayed at home he would buy me a Triumph Spitfire. I went to see one in red in Robin's Dad's garage; he sold motor vehicles. I was spellbound. I should have just opted for Manchester and would have been delighted with this. I ended up sitting the Oxford entrance exams for Medicine. This went well and I got an interview. The interview also went well and I was asked the difference between Entropy and Enthalpy. Because I was always reading, any science-based topic, I was able to tell my interviewer. Sadly it was not to be. There were four places and seven had been invited for interview. I think the Manchester Grammar lads had all done and got their A-levels – I was yet to take mine. I think all four places went to them. Even worse, all my other choices for University deserted me and I ended up going to Cardiff, my last choice, which was the furthest away and would take me 6 hours on the train door to door.

I was devastated as I knew that my dog was not getting any younger and neither was my dad! I had this fear that when I returned – if I returned – 5 years later things would be very different. I did my best to come home as often as I could but the journey on the train was difficult. Because I had accepted my place so late all the student accommodation was booked and I ended up in a Methodist hall of residence in Penarth, which is a few miles out of Cardiff. These were the days of Tiger bay and Barry Island. Penarth, however, was very 'middle England' and very upmarket. To this day it's wonderful and there are super walks along the coastline. International House, where I stayed, is now a nursing home but is still there and only changed a little from the outside.

Towards the end of my time at Eccles College, for a few weeks, I'd been dating a really nice girl. We'd met at a course at Manchester University. She was a pupil at Urmston Grammar. I remember she had stunning green eyes. We went out a few times. The catalyst of course to asking girls out was the ability to say to them "What time would you like me to pick you up?" Being able to borrow my Mum's little red Mini and also, without doubt, to be able to drive was a real boost. I'd started learning as soon as I was 17. I wanted a motorbike but my mum forbade it as the boy at the back of us had sadly just been killed on one. She flatly refused but did say I could learn to drive as soon as I was able. I remember I passed on Friday 13th June, 1975. It was my first test and I remember someone pulling out without warning in front of me just under Strangeways prison. Mercifully I reacted quickly, but I thought I must definitely have failed. The examiner however told me that I had passed. I was busily removing the L-Plates from my mum's car. This massive truck stopped, blocking the whole road. The driver wound his window down and shouted "Well done, kid!" and drove off.

My aunt was visiting us at the time. She asked me if I felt like a man and at first I didn't know what she meant but I realised later than something had changed. It gave me the confidence to start asking girls out. Moreover, at weekends I would put Sabre in the back of the car and we would drive up to Rivington. He would sit in the back of the car for hours and used to love his trips in the car – especially as there were no back doors for him to fall through!

Around this time my Dad retired. The local GPs all started out as single-handers. Workload was extreme and in the early days of course there was no out-of-hours handover. They would all work 7 days a week and 24 hrs a day. I remember Dad would run three surgeries a day and also do Saturday and Sunday. With time, the local GPs used to co-operate. Even this was fraught with problems. My Dad was phoned one day by Dr Campbell, one of his local colleagues. He was feeling dreadful and asked whether my Dad could cover the night for him. "Of course, Ian, and I hope you are feeling better soon." My Dad thought no more about this until the following day when Mum was talking to our neighbour Mrs Lennard who was very much into her golf and was either Lady Captain or was soon to be made so at Worsley Golf Club. She just happened to mention to my Mum that she'd met up with Dr Campbell in the golf club the night before and that he was really on form and was buying everyone drinks. My Mum somewhat naively said that this couldn't be possible as he was at home and had gone to bed. Mrs Lennard said that he was in top form, was in a very good mood and was there all evening!

Dr Campbell in particular was a real character. One day he was phoned by a patient who told him that his wife was hysterical and asked what he should do. Dr Campbell advised him that he should throw a bucket of cold water over her. This he promptly did and I am unable to say what happened next. I can say that if we were to advise this today, then the GMC would be very keen to hear of it and would expect any GP to appear in front of them in order to explain himself!

Many times at weekends we would visit Dr Borkin. He was a lovely man and right from an early age he and his family would be very courteous to the four of us when we visited. Even in those days, however, the poor man was very stressed and again like the GPs of the day would work very hard. He was also the Police Surgeon and would be called out at night for them in addition to his own rota. Worsley road as one turns right on Patricroft bridge as one passes Tesco on the left was very different in days gone by. It was very narrow and had sharp blind bends. My Mum would always recount a tale where one day Dr Borkin overtook her at great speed along this section of road and I think of this as I drive along there to this day, though of course it is much wider and has been made a lot less dangerous.

Eccles Health Centre was formed around this time and six local single-handed GPs were invited to close their individual surgeries often running out of small premises, and move there. It was brand new with more facilities and of course was the way forward. The Government are still intent on closing down single-handed practices though I am not at all sure that it has anything to do with patient dissatisfaction with such GPs or premises, but there we are.

My Dad was never as happy at Eccles Health Centre as he'd been on his own and put in place plans to retire a short time later. I think he found it difficult to get home and pray. GPs in those days would go on and on and when walking my dog I would often see Dr Samson and his wife. Dr Samson worked down in the New Lane surgery, and please correct me if I am wrong, but I think this went on to become Springfield house. Anyway, I believe he was still working into his eighties.

I had had a few dates with Diane, who was the girl with the gorgeous green eyes. We would often go out with another male friend of mine, Dave. It became clear that this friend was greatly attracted to Diane – and vice-versa! It wasn't anyone's fault. I am sure he was much 'cooler' and more handsome than I was. There was no point in jumping up and down about the inevitable and very soon after this they started dating.

Not long after this, however, I was at the Eccles College disco at the Lancastrian Hall and sitting next to the four of us lads were four super girls from Adelphi house. In those days Adelphi house girls were taught by the FCJ – Faithful Companions of Jesus and, as you'll realise, all the girls were devout Catholics. Not that this was ever a problem; it certainly wasn't something that my Mum or Dad were unhappy with and we all had a great time. I guess with my background it would have been a bit two-faced for my mum or dad to be picky about whom I dated!

Four of us lads and a few of the girls started going out as a group of friends. I thought this worked really well as, or so I believed, we got on very well and had a really nice time. Sadly, as is the way with things, my friend wasn't happy with the group arrangement. He wanted to ask one of the girls out and did so. I think she turned him down. This caused the arrangement to fracture a short time later.

My sister had met the girls and suggested to me that she thought one of them was stunning and that I should ask her out. Jane was quite correct; she was a lovely girl with a 'shock' of blonde hair and great legs and we started going out a short time later. Just before we did so we were talking about how things had started to fall apart and that song "Don't throw it all away" by Gary Benson had just been released and she used to quote from it. I remember my first date with Rita the stunning blonde. My Dad was still up when I got in. He asked me about my date and then said something along the lines of "Oh well, when you get married!" I was shocked by this and reminded him it was our first date. He then said that marriage was always a gamble and that I should not leave it too late to get married, like he had!

A while later we'd been going out for almost a year. Rita's friend, she lived in a house facing Rita's, was also going out with a lad and we would see them as I dropped her off at her house. She told me one night that her friend had been given an ultimatum by her boyfriend that if she didn't sleep with him, then he'd dump her. She asked me what I thought about that and I said that it wasn't very nice and that she should dump him. I asked her what she thought about it and she then told me that she'd be okay with it as long as he understood that if something went wrong then the boy would have to marry her. I was eighteen and had an interview at Oxford the following day. So despite it being a really good offer, it suddenly and catastrophically crystallised things for me. I thought it best if we ended it as I would not really be in a position to form a serious relationship if I was leaving for Med School. Rita was not very happy, but so many years away from home lay before me and I wasn't going to use her or anyone else for that matter. I could only think it was in her best interests too.

During my first year at Med School one of the students got his girlfriend pregnant. She was also a medical student. She dropped down a year and I would sometimes see them at parties with their baby. It seemed at the age of 19 or 20 this was a great burden to bear, especially if one takes into account the stresses of the medicine course which was incredibly intense and stressful. They stayed together but for many of us, though not all, their example was a very good disincentive to engaging in intimate relationships.

Chapter IX

WNSM

When all was said and done, the following September I started in Cardiff at the Welsh National School of Medicine. The 125 (HST) train service began the same day and I managed to catch a glimpse of one that had come from Reading on the line west to South Wales. Cardiff was a super Medical School, but I was a long way from home. I was also very lonely and very hard up for money. I would save all my money to finance train tickets home to see my dog or to save up for a little car. As my Dad had retired by this time I got a grant to go towards my living expenses but it was still hard going. Each day I would get some lunch in the student union. The cheapest thing on the menu was black pudding and beans (Heinz not butter!) for 22p. I had this every day for three years!

One day I was in the student union with my beans and two slices of black pudding. There was an empty seat facing this chap who was eating Spaghetti Bolognese. I asked him if I could sit down. He must have been quite well off because this was a more expensive option. I noticed that after eating a few mouthfuls he pushed it away from him and left. A few minutes later someone asked me if that seat was taken. I told the newcomer that I thought that he'd gone. I didn't notice that he was not carrying anything. He sat down, now facing me, and without any further ado, ate what was left of the Bolognese! This brought home to me quite acutely that being hard up was a relative thing and after this I didn't see myself as being hard up – I just had to be careful with my money and this by and large was to set the scene from that day onwards. This was to be tested when at the start of one term my grant did not arrive from Salford; the lady in the office could not have cared less. I had no money at all and for those first few weeks and I had to be very careful. The banks in those days were quite suspicious of students and I think I got a book token when I joined the bank in Penarth, but no overdraft. I was given a cheque book but could not have a cheque guarantee card. This too was a good discipline and it meant once again that every penny would have to be accounted for and spent wisely.

I was still very lonely but whenever I went home I would meet up with Patsy my friend from Clarendon road. She would introduce me to all her friends who were all super, clever and witty girls. I was often to be found in the Last Drop in Bolton with five or six girls who had become my friends too! Occasionally Robin would contact me and he would always have interesting places to go like the Playboy club in Manchester. This was really exciting. We would have a couple of drinks there and sometimes something to eat but of course I could never afford to gamble. I was amazed by the young women who worked the tables who wore really high shoes (sorry) and would walk up and down as they ran the tables. They would all walk on clear plastic mats in order to protect the carpet. Of course I could never afford to ask one out and in any case most of them would have been a foot taller than I was anyway!

I had some great friends at International House. The nice thing is that we all did different things. One was doing Accountancy, another Pharmacy, another Music and so on. We also met lots of people from all over the world. The journalists' course, the TEFL and port management courses were especially popular. We would also be taught lots of foreign languages. Sometimes, sadly, this would be no more than a few words and in truth not always nice ones! I can swear in lots of different languages and, it has to be said, the meaning is not that nice. One chap was a very keen Welsh nationalist and would be forever teaching us more and more imaginative ways of insulting English people. This for him would reach fever proportions whenever England were playing Wales at the Arms Park. We used to dread his coming back if Wales lost as he would be in mourning for days on end.

As medical students doing our Orthopaedics, we were sometimes taught by JPR Williams who, in those days, was revered in Welsh Rugby circles. He used to have long sideburns and rumour had it that these covered scars where his face had been raked a few times by opponents' boots.

Each day we would walk up to the station in Penarth and catch the 8:07 to Cardiff, then I would walk up to the University. When people asked me where I was from and I told them Manchester they would all laugh and invariably say, "It rains a lot in Manchester, doesn't it?" Every day it would rain in Cardiff. I have never encountered so much rain. I would be drenched all day sitting in lectures. After a few weeks of this I would agree with them that it rained in Manchester but informed them that it did not rain as much as in Cardiff.

One winter I had been home for the weekend and on the Sunday night it had snowed so much in Cardiff that there were twelve-foot snowdrifts. The trains to Penarth had all been cancelled and I could not afford a taxi. I found a couple of friends who lived at that time in Dingle or Cogan which were not quite as far as Penarth which was about 5 miles by road. More recently they have renovated the whole of the sea-facing frontage and one can get from Penarth to Cardiff fairly quickly. We set off walking. I was coming down with flu and feeling dreadful. It was very late and the snow was really thick. One chap stopped on the road in a white Triumph TR6. He said he wanted a passenger to put a bit more weight in the car. My friends insisted that I get in as I had furthest to go. The driver apologised for the heater being on full blast but he was trying to keep the windows clear. I sat there shivering and told him not to worry. When I got to International House I was feeling dreadful. My friend brought me some cherry brandy that his mum and dad had sent him and suggested that it was for medicinal purposes. I slept the night round and awoke feeling much better and to find that Penarth was cut off because of the snowdrifts. A few days later I found the parked white TR6 and placed a 4 pack of cans on the roof with a little note of my thanks.

Around this time, in Penarth, several cars were randomly attacked by someone who poured paint stripper on the bodywork. Students were stopped by the Police who then asked them if they could look in their bags. We didn't think it could be anyone from International House as they were all a nice group of people. During the long walk from International House to the station one would pass many fine houses. Upon reading a book about Guy Gibson I realised that his future wife had lived in one of those houses and I must have passed it a hundred times.

Some of the students had very wealthy parents. In those days the Persians, as they were known then, were particularly wealthy. This was the days of the Shah. One lad drove round Cardiff in a Porsche. There was someone stealing from the tuck shop in International House, which had an honesty box. One night we lay in wait and were really shocked to discover who it was. We impressed upon him that he was to repay as much of the money as he could and he was never to do it again or we would ‘grass’ on him.

My friend Albert had a habit, if we left our bags at reception while we went to breakfast, of putting all the magazines from the reception desk into our college bags to make them much heavier and if we weren’t on the ball we would discover that we’d carried into college a load of magazines. I’m not sure if the Police did find the phantom paint stripper but in any event the attacks soon died down. Albert’s other favourite trick, when he was in the library, was to place library books in people’s bags. As soon as they left the alarms would go off and they would be found with lots of library books. Mercifully he never had occasion to do this to me as I had moved to my clinical years at the Heath Hospital by this time. This at first meant an extra train ride but I was almost able to afford my little car.

By the end of second year we had second MB, which is where a lot of students are filtered out. Second MB exams are thus very important. I had made the acquaintance of a nice young woman who was of mixed race, half French and half Columbian. She would pop into my room at night and make me coffee. She had supplies of wonderful Columbian coffee which to this day causes a smile whenever I see it. We would not get into anything too passionate but she would stay talking for hours. At midnight she would sneak back to her room and said that she'd better go as I had to study! I was so shattered by then I went straight to bed. I think the distraction caused me to take my eye off the ball and though I passed my second MB my Mum was especially scared as I told her I wasn't sure I was going to come home that summer as I was besotted by this girl. My friend Jake, however, saved me. He saw us both in Caerphilly. The Queen was in Caerphilly that day and we had a trip out. He asked me who I was with. I told him and he said, "Oh, I thought that was your mother!"

Suddenly and somehow the spell was broken. I went home and returned that September having passed my second MB; she was going out with another boy.

Some years later when Jake and his wife visited us in Monton I reminded him of this and he and his wife had a great chuckle. I told him that I always meant to ask him if my Mum had phoned him to try to get me back on track or if it's something he just said spontaneously! He didn't answer!

Each summer I would get a job and earn as much as I could. Starting from my O-level year I worked at Trafford warehouses and also at Makro. The lady next door had a nice new Mini and she told me that in a year or two she would sell it and I could have first refusal. I worked and saved as much as I could. The temptation at Makro in particular was to spend one's wages in the store afterwards and I had to be very disciplined. I was also very accident prone and I am amazed that Makro didn't sack me. Things came to a head especially when I was working on non-food end control loading customers' trolleys. One chap bought this vast bag of Winalot, he must have had a pet shop or a kennels because I have never seen one so big. I think it contained 56 lbs of dog biscuit. He approached end-control with this on his trolley. I asked him to please leave it on the trolley, as it was so large. He insisted on picking it up. I rushed to help him and grabbed it. It must have been nicked on the metal shelves that were at end control. The whole thing then 'unzipped' around the middle just as I grabbed it. The whole contents were then deposited around me as I stood there and within seconds I was standing in the middle of a mountain of Winalot.

My worse crime however was not to 'read the signs' if the store was quiet. One of my friends advised me to get a brush at such times. I couldn't find one and so I just stood there waiting for customers. Out of the corner of my eye I saw the Manager in his glass-walled office pick up the phone. Within seconds I was transferred to food, goods receiving. It was a baking hot summer's day. I was asked to shovel a mountain of rotting fruit and vegetables into this massive skip so that it would be disposed of. I was there until it was the end of my shift. I did not get any relief or a break. I did however learn two very important lessons. One was to keep busy especially when the store was quiet and the second was a warning as to what could happen to me if I failed my exams!

That summer, I was 21, I had managed to save £1,600. The lady next door unfortunately changed her mind about selling her car. A new Mini 1000 was £2,025 and I did not have enough. My Dad said he would give me the extra and I was delighted. Although it was only a small-engined car (in fact 998cc) it was perfect for getting home. If I stuck to a steady 50mph it would take 4 hours and do 50 miles to the gallon. One could not speed as petrol consumption and thus costs would climb. I cannot see what all the fuss is about with these modern cars. For sure they are very much faster but driven carefully, my Mini would still return great fuel consumption. The journey was a bit boring and once or twice I nearly fell asleep. I used to take the A449 if I could. This had a lot of roundabouts on it. One evening, heading back to Penarth, I must have fallen asleep as I woke to see the danger chevrons of the roundabout just in front of my bonnet. Mercifully nobody was in the roundabout. I heaved on the steering wheel and managed just to avoid crashing into the warning sign. The car skidded round the roundabout, but it had shaken me so much at least it woke me up! My friend as a junior doctor working in Birmingham was driving home late one night back to Manchester. He was woken by the sound of his windscreen cracking as his car went *under* the truck in front of him! On one occasion a sports car drove in front of me and really slowed down. I moved out to overtake him whereupon he just sped up. This went on for miles and eventually I just had to stay behind him and let him dictate the speed until he turned off.

I retained my interest in electronics and made a digital rev counter for my car, which had a line of square LEDs which lit up progressively as the revs climbed. At the higher revs they turned red. Such solid-state devices were rare in those days as meters and dials were almost universal. I also assembled an electronic ignition which one made up from a kit. This would clip to the coil and was said to make the spark more efficient and the fuel consumption better.

Although the kit came together really well, there must have been a 'dry' joint somewhere that had not been soldered properly. The engine could conk out without warning and on many occasions when, mercifully, I was only on the A449 and it was pretty quiet, I would have to get out of the car, furtle under the bonnet and switch the electronic ignition off so that the car's standard ignition could take over. Not surprisingly the kit also came with breakerless contacts, which would replace the points. The trouble was this meant that one could not revert back to the car's standard equipment so, I never plucked up the courage to take the final step.

It was also true that my lucky streak (or foolish if you prefer!) had not deserted me. I knew that I would have to keep my car for some years and decided, as people did in those days, to underseal it. In order to do this one usually chose a bitumen-like compound. Thinking I knew better, I chose red lead, which was the stuff they used to paint ship's hulls with. I put the car up on ramps and then went underneath. I started painting. I had not realised just how toxic the fumes were and although I was outside I had not got a mask on. After about 20 minutes as the fumes overcame me, I felt really sick and started to vomit uncontrollably. I got out from under the car but I would often wonder what would have happened if I'd stayed under there any longer. At least I had the presence of mind not to do any more!

I was finishing at Makro and my little yellow Mini, TTD 75T was in the car park. One always remembers one's first car. One of the boys at end control had bought a new motorbike. All the students and staff went out to look at his motorbike, including me. The following day one of the permanent staff, who was a nice lady and who'd been there many years, told me she'd seen me getting into my little car and that I had not said anything. By this time I had reverted to being my quiet, unassuming self – the person whom I believe that I would have been had that lady not rushed out from her house to meet up with me when I was six. My battles were all but over by this time and all I had to do was to keep up with my work. I used to try to be in the top 50 out of 150 at Med school and nearly always managed this. Otherwise I could let some of my more competitive edge calm a bit and concentrate on being a nicer person.

One more lesson awaited me however and sadly it too was a painful one. A few years earlier the lady who lived next door, Mrs Dean, came round. I was a surly teenager at this time. When she'd gone my mum was upset. She told me that I should have stood when a lady entered the room. I could tell that she was disappointed in me. I am sure that I must have given her a load of cheek that I never knew such a thing, but I was stung by her disappointment, which of course I remember to this day. Some years later, I must have been 18 or 19 and it must have been before I got my Mini as I was on the train to Cardiff. Wolverhampton was always a bit of a flash point. There was never any trouble but a typical incident occurred when the train was packed and I, along with many others, was standing. It was one of the old compartment trains that were still in use but were being phased out. There was a seat next to a young Indian lady, wearing a Sari, in one of the compartments. Two lads were in the corridor and one said to the other that there was a seat next to the Asian lady and suggested that he sit there. The other boy then launched in to all the reasons why he did not want to sit next to this lady. He then told his friend to go and sit there and for similar reasons and also after spouting a bit he refused. I nearly asked them if they would mind if I pushed past them in order to go and sit there but I was not keen to antagonise them and was also not keen to be talked about in a similar fashion. I would always keep my head down and keep myself to myself when we went through Wolverhampton.

A couple of weeks later I was on the train and it was one of the more modern open carriages. I was sitting at this little table on the train and was getting some revision done. My friend's dad was a radiographer and in those days the 'plates' were packed in these large sheets of amber-coloured paper. These were super for revision as one could record so much information on them. For instance, I had one on which I'd drawn a really large table showing all the muscle insertions, names and actions for all the muscles in the forearm. I would read these and many more whilst I was on the train in order to learn them. The train had just stopped at Wolverhampton. I looked up and in front of me was the most gorgeous young woman I had ever set eyes on. She was smiling at me. She asked me if the seat facing me was taken. I was spellbound and managed to voice somehow that it wasn't. She struggled with her bag, placing it in the overhead rack. I was fixed to my seat wondering if in the rest of the journey I would be able to pluck up enough courage to actually speak to her.

At that moment a tall, older chap, who had obviously been distressed by what he saw, came over to her. He told her that there was a seat a little further down the carriage and he thought she'd be much more comfortable down there. He grabbed her bag and with a tiny smile she left, never to be seen again.

I was ashamed, and it was a cruel lesson. I would love to be able to tell you that he was just a racist and that he didn't want this angel on earth sitting facing some grubby half-caste. That is the thing when one opens the 'colour' debate. It is easy to blame someone else for your wrong behaviour or to say that you have only behaved in that way because of others' assumptions of you. I suspect the truth was that he was incensed that I had not got off my bottom to help this pleasant young woman who had struggled with her case. Remember please that this was probably about 1976. The world was very different then. I know today people would not think twice about watching a girl on a train struggling with a bag. At that time, however, things were very different. I had used an excuse to avoid my engaging in correct behaviour. If only I could have turned the clock back those 5 minutes – that would be all that I would need to get off my fat bottom and to treat the young woman correctly. Sadly that option is not open to us and people would feel what they felt, and remember what they saw, in that moment. If any of you know that young woman then, please, give her my apology! They say that those who don't learn from their mistakes are compelled to repeat them and I should have learned from the incident when our neighbour came round. Not that I didn't learn however from this second incident and reminder. I resolved to be a better, more caring and more perceptive person in future.

Another thing conflated quickly from an event that had happened a short time before. My Dad would take the odd cine film and we have some footage from when Jane and I were young and, of course, the time we got Sabre. We had a little cottage in Anglesey and I was larking in the garden. My Dad was taking some film. Some years later as we were viewing this. He said words that I always remember. “My, John, you were so happy then.” This was not meant as any form of criticism; Dad wasn’t that sort of person, he would never engage in some sort of snide comment. He meant it quite literally. It set me wondering, however, if I came over as a person who rarely smiled and rarely looked happy. I resolved to do better and even today each of my waking moments I think of such things.

The third leg of the tripod that formed much of my attitude to the world had come many years before. I was a little boy at primary school. I had a new raincoat, which was in navy blue. I think the three Dean boys had bought them and they looked so wonderful I asked my Mum if I could have one. Most important of all it had a secret key which was a little plastic key on a chain. If you fished in the left hand pocket, behind the secret flap you would find the special key which was made of bright red plastic. I am sure it seems pretty underwhelming by the delights that our kids have to call upon these days, but to me any many others it was simply amazing. One afternoon I came running out of school and my mum was talking to Mr Wernick, Robin’s dad. I flashed my secret key as I came running. “Look, Mummy, it’s a secret key!” Mr Wernick turned to my Mum and said “Oh, so he does talk then!” Without doubt I was a very quiet little boy, but I would have always taken the view that there was a lot going on inside! It seems, perhaps unsurprisingly, that people do not see this unless you show them. They don’t have the time or inclination to wonder about views and thoughts you hold within. I decided to up my game. To this day you will find me doing my best to engage with every single person I meet.

Just last week the four of us were in Newcastle for Lottie's graduation. We had ordered a taxi to take us to the city centre and the degree ceremony. Lottie had forgotten her student pass and raced back to her room to get it. The taxi driver was really grumpy. I was doing my best to engage with him but without any success; he remained taciturn. As we got out of the taxi, the girls laughed and said "Dad, well done, you tried really hard with that man!"

Anyway, once again I am drifting. The years at International House were good ones. I went home in my little car as often as I was able. I tried to get home every other weekend. Of course I missed out on the student life in the residence whilst I did this but did my best to try and get work done and also chill with my friends.

It has to be said that we were naughty. Not in a horrible way but certainly in a mischievous way. There was the speaker under the bed. We sent a wire round the outside of the building and placed a speaker under someone's bed. We'd found out that one room had a master key that would open anyone's room. When the lad was downstairs we placed a speaker under his bed and when he went to sleep and through the microphone we'd set up started the sound of clanking chains and ghost whispers. He took it in good part. My friend Albert decided that all new students should be doused with a bucket of water. We waited on the fourth floor and leant out of the window that looked down on the entrance, full bucket in hand. The new student was unloading the car with his dad. In he hopped, away went the bucket and with pinpoint accuracy – it covered his dad! I must admit the warden knew just who to look for. We went down to apologise and his dad, although dripping wet, took it in very good spirit. Then there was the evening that a political party invited us to spend the evening with them at their local branch. Two were in the front seat and three of us in the back. This guy who was driving us was definitely worse for wear. Our friend Meriel was sitting next to him and was wearing a skirt. He started rubbing her thigh as he was driving along. Albert was sitting next to Meriel in the front. He looked past her to address the driver. “Excuse me, Sir, have you been drinking?”

Mercifully it was a short journey and Meriel managed to cling to Albert for much of it. In the end we had a nice evening and I think for the first and only time in my life I won the raffle of a large basket of fruit, which I shared with everyone. As I think I said, I am not a routinely lucky person, but when I have needed luck – to save my arm or my life – it has not deserted me.

A further prank that we were wholly responsible for was the waterbombs from the roof. We’d found a way up via the lift housing to get onto the roof. In sunny afternoons people would be sitting outside. We would make the water bombs using Origami (or perhaps misusing Origami!) and then we’d drop them on to those below.

The most horrific was the man in the mask outside the girls’ rooms on Halloween. Poor Zohra from Libya was just closing her curtains and then she saw him on the flat roof outside their rooms. She screamed and screamed and screamed again. The chap who was playing the ‘masked man’ quickly threw away his walking stick, scarpered off the roof and we all retired pretty quickly to our rooms. Once again the warden was very patient and over the next few days quiet apologies were made to Zohra who saw the funny side.

Not forgetting the Xmas party. We put so much alcohol in the fruit punch that it was a pretty toxic mix. One of the Persian girls who, without doubt, should not have been drinking alcohol informed us that she knew there was alcohol in it but she didn't care! One of my friends announced, "No smoking near the punch, it will explode."

International House was home to many students from all over the world. Christina was a journalist on the course in Cardiff. She was half Chinese and half Portugese. My friend Albert, himself Chinese Malay, told me that such 'branches everywhere', as he put it, mixes were frowned upon in the Chinese community. Of course my whole life had taught me this. And yet the girl was absolutely stunning. Moreover, she always had an entourage of men who hung on every word that she uttered and although I never actually got to speak with her I was vicariously proud of her – she was so impressive.

Then there was the PhD student from Argentina who used to go for a long, long walk at the same time each night. Many months later Ashish the Chemistry lecturer told me that the student would meet her married lover on each of these occasions.

One of the worst things happened to Albert. There were two bathrooms on each floor. He went diagonally out of his room and straight into the bathroom and reversed the journey on the way back. This particular night the first bathroom was occupied and so he went to the one further down the corridor. On coming out automatically he took his usual diagonal and, without further ado, had now barged into the wrong room. There on the bed in flagrante delicto was the ambassador's wife, from a country that I'd better not name, and the Turkish guy. Albert quickly beat a retreat and in telling the tale later could only conclude that he'd wished that the ground had opened and swallowed him up!

Of course what went on was no business of ours, although a short time later the Turkish guy rented a 26" colour television, which was on with the volume turned up, each evening that he wasn't in her room, on the other side of my wall when I was trying to get some studying done.

We certainly saw life and also many different cultures. The chaps from Mombassa, who were doing the Port Management course in Cardiff, were lovely people. They taught me a bit of Swahili. By contrast, the lads from Papua New Guinea, who were all married, were constantly on the look out for prostitutes. If the warden had found out they would have been expelled. A Methodist Minister came in each week and ran prayers in the chapel. One of my friends, Dyfed, who was the keen rugby supporter, told me that he did not go in the TV room for the first six months because he thought it was the Chapel!

There was also a group of Chinese doctors who were on the chest course at Llandaff hospital. We were fascinated and horrified watching them eat their fried eggs in the morning. They would somehow pick up the whole egg and perch it on their knife and fork, from where it was offered up to the mouth. The whole quivering thing would then be somehow hoovered up by suction as the entire egg would be eaten in one go. It was really horrible to watch yet strangely fascinating.

Upon learning that I was a medical student people would start bringing medical problems to me. One of the Papua New Guineans entered into a long conversation with me at breakfast to ask me why his manly appendage was not as hard as he would like it. I resisted the temptation to tell him that it was perhaps because his wife was at home and perhaps consorting with other girls might have something to do with it! When the chap from Tonga left they found hundreds of empty beer cans stuffed under his bed. Being a Methodist Hall, alcohol was banned.

In the fullness of time we were about to enter Final Year. At this time students are encouraged to travel the world and look at alternative health care systems. They then work in local hospitals in that area. One chap went to California as one of the surgeons was into sky-diving. Others went to the Bahamas, Canada and Africa. I was so hard up and also keen to spend time at home as the academic terms by this time were very long with only a few weeks holiday each year. I applied to Hope Hospital in the surgical department. This was a great attachment for me as I did my best to get stuck in and help the junior doctors, who in those days were referred to as junior housemen, on the surgical wards.

One of the housemen had an interview in London and she asked me if I would cover the ward for her for 48 hours. As soon as she went, all hell was let loose. It was the busiest 48 hours of my life. So many patients were plunged into extreme ill-health as soon as she'd gone. I started around 7am and by midnight I went for my first and only wee, having not had anything to eat or drink in this time. One of the surgeons came to check on his poorly patient who'd had a hind-quarter amputation because of gangrene. The patient was desperately unwell and the amputation was the only way to save his life. The surgeon, Mr Marcusson, stopped me on the stairs to ask me how he was. I was able to give him a detailed but brief summary, including key blood tests, from the top of my head while we stood talking on the stairs. Before I left, Mr Marcusson asked me if I would be kind enough to consider him when I applied for my own House jobs. I told him that I would be honoured. Hospitals in Wales would tend to favour Cardiff graduates. The system is very different now but in those days it was very hard to break out of Wales because as one might expect Manchester hospitals would favour Manchester graduates and so on. I was thus very lucky to be given such an opportunity in a large teaching hospital.

Although it was still some time before finals I already had another house job lined up. I'd done a student attachment in North Wales and again, before I left, the consultant asked me by way of formal letter if I would be his houseman. In truth North Wales was regarded as a bit of a professional backwater as there were no teaching hospitals such as in South Wales or Hope Hospital. However, the local people were lovely and I got to do so many procedures, things like chest drains, lumbar punctures, liver biopsies and kidney biopsies – that young qualified doctors today could only dream of. I accepted his offer.

Suddenly finals were upon us. The Heath, which was the main teaching hospital just up the road from Cardiff, ran revision courses in the evenings which were excellent but, staying in Penarth, it was difficult for me to get there. This was a big mistake as many hints were apparently dropped as to what would be appearing in the finals exams. In any event things went smoothly apart from the final long case, which was a disaster. Failing this would mean failing finals. I phoned my mum and dad that night very upset as I thought I might have failed. My dad came on the phone which was a rare thing, the only other time he'd done this was one Friday I wanted to drive home in thick snow and my Mum said it was too dangerous. She was so concerned that she put Dad on the phone and so of course I stayed in Cardiff. Anyway, coming back to my finals, my Dad said that I wasn't to worry. If I had failed then it was best for me to come home and I could always do accountancy. I reminded my brother in law, who is an accountant, of this in my wedding speech some years later.

In the event I got through. My Mum, Rodney and sister-in-law came to my graduation but sadly not my Dad. Prince Charles gave out the certificates and what a wonderful person he was. He was very warm, very friendly and seemed genuinely delighted to speak to as many people and particularly students as possible. Meeting him up close one-to-one was instructive; so much is written in the papers, but I was deeply impressed by him. I know that he had a bad press when his marriage to Diana failed, but I can only speak as I found and he was friendly, attentive and very interested to talk to all of us medical students.

On the evening that results were announced I was in the Sully Inn, which is another posh place just beyond Penarth. I was with a couple of friends from International House. I heard a voice behind me, "Congratulations, Dr Behardien." Apart from the time when the Chemistry teacher told me off in the labs at Eccles College for having my lab coat open, this was the first time I had been so addressed and it felt strange but wonderful. I turned to see one of my contemporaries in the same pub and I congratulated him too. It felt a bit like the time at 17 when I'd passed my driving test and my Aunt had asked me if I felt like a man.

Chapter X

House Jobs

My contract in North Wales mentioned the Ysbyty Gwynedd, which was the brand new hospital. Unfortunately, this wasn't ready and I would work at the older hospital, the C&A in the centre of Bangor. It has long since been pulled down and I think now is a supermarket car park. This was an old hospital. We would work a 1 in 3 which meant that we were on-call maybe one or two nights in the week and one weekend in three. The nurses would often, by way of polite conversation, ask us what time we were finishing and at the time of asking it might be a Friday morning. We would say 6pm Monday if we were on-call that weekend. They would then say, "Yes, but what time do you finish?" It was hard to make them understand that we would be working continuously from the Friday morning when they'd asked us until that time on the next Monday. If you were lucky and the hospital was quiet then you might get an hour or two of sleep but this was a variable thing. I do have some sympathy with the junior doctors of today. When I started at Hope the pretty administrator told me that I had two contracts. One detailed the Class A UMT (units of medical time) and the other contract the Class B. I was told I would be paid for both. Before I got too excited I realised that the Class B UMT was the one that applied after 6pm, all through the night and all weekends and would be paid at one third of the A; please note that is not time and a third but one third of time! I still have my payslips from those early days and it seems that the junior doctors have been 'put on' at least since 1981 when I started. To be fair, they no longer have to work continuous shifts as we had to. On many occasions in the middle of the night, when I had gone cross-eyed with exhaustion, I'd be struggling to get drips and needles inserted just when the patient's condition was most critical!

At the C&A I had a nice, large room; not that there was any time to relax there as the packed work schedule would keep one busy. One night I was asleep and the bleep went off. I put on the light and got up. I think I'd collapsed on the bed still in my white coat. I realised that the floor was moving. I blinked a couple of times thinking it must be my vision that was playing me up. I then realised that the whole floor really was moving! It was like one of those Egyptian horror movies, filmed in the accursed tomb, as the floor was covered in cockroaches. There were thousands of them; the floor was completely covered with this seething mass. This is why it appeared to be moving. The following day I asked housekeeping if they could find me another room. There was only one room left and it was actually directly off one of the wards up a short flight of stairs. It was very tiny; when the wardrobe door was opened it came up against the bed and one couldn't get out. However, it was clean and dry. As I was getting my stuff from my old room I noted that there was a packet of biscuits of uncertain age under the wardrobe and most likely these had been attracting the cockroaches. The other advantage of my new little room is that I could be on the ward within seconds. When the consultant had arranged for one of his friends to be admitted there one night he asked me to look out for him even though I wasn't on call.

Of course, I was lonely again and as soon as I'd qualified and started my first job at Hope Hospital my dog had died. His back paws had gone and the poor soul could not walk. He was really breathless. We went to a really cruel vet who shouted at me for placing Sabre on the bench in his waiting room. I said that he was just so heavy I didn't think I could pick him up off the floor. He told me that he could not do anything and he would have to put him to sleep. Sabre was trembling. He used to hate going to the vet's. The cruel man got the injection ready and Sabre was shaking. I just said to him in those closing seconds, "We are going home." Sabre of course understood all these words and brightened visibly and stopped shaking just as he passed away in my arms. My Mum who came with me told the Vet that he should not be a vet as he was too uncaring and that her son had just qualified as a junior doctor and would never treat his patients that way! We went home and I buried Sabre in the back garden, not wishing to leave his body with such an unfeeling man. I had never been so upset in my life. My brother in law turned up; I just couldn't stop crying and without a word being spoken he just helped me to dig a hole large enough and deep enough to bury Sabre.

A few weeks later my Dad died. I turned 24 in the December and my Dad died the following March/April. I was doing my housejob in Wales but had come home for the weekend. My Mum came into my room to say that she couldn't wake him and I realised straight away that he'd had a massive stroke and he would be unlikely to recover from such a thing. Sure enough within a few days he passed away without ever regaining consciousness. There were so many things that I'd want to ask him and so many wonderful things that I'd want to show him. He was a caring and devout Muslim and I think he would be saddened by the events of the modern world.

Some months before he died my Dad, as the devout were required to do, went on the Haj, which is the holy pilgrimage to Mecca. He told me that he had to do this before he died. We were not to worry about him as if he died whilst making this journey his faith held that he would enter Paradise immediately. It was something he was determined to do even though, in truth, the three of us did not want him to go; feeling that something dreadful was about to happen. Sadly, as soon as he got to Saudi Arabia he was robbed of absolutely everything apart from the clothes on his back. He had no money and no passport. The consul in Riyadh took pity on him and believed his version of events. He arranged for a new passport and for my Dad to be flown back to England. He was deeply affected by these cruel events.

The song by "Mike and the Mechanics" entitled "The Living Years" always reminds me of this time. Our two girls are now 22 and 25 and with a little more luck I am keen to be around for a few more years, but I do my best to not leave things unsaid and questions unanswered.

My sister told me some years later that Dad was praying to die. He didn't feel well and had problems with his diabetes and his vision was poor and was affected by painful arthritis and his experiences on the pilgrimage had deeply affected him. Nevertheless, he was only 72, which I guess is young seen through today's lens. In any event his prayers were answered within 7 days and he passed away in the night with no pain and no suffering. A couple of weeks before he died he asked me if I would look after my Mum and at that time, not really knowing why he'd asked me such a question, I promised him that I would.

A few days later, going back to work in Wales was especially hard. I remember that he died without making a will. My brother-in-law had frozen all the accounts for probate and my poor Mum had all these bills rolling in, but no money. I still had my old account from Penarth and also a new one at a local bank. I signed two cheques and put them on the telly. I told Mum that she could draw £267 pounds on one and up to £84 on the other, this being all the money I had. The local bank staff were very helpful to her as was a local accountant who had a little office above the Drop-Inn in Monton. They are still my accountants today even though they closed the Monton office and concentrated on the Bolton and Darwen ones.

Spring and Summer were coming in and if I wasn't on call I would go for long walks, mainly on the beaches of Anglesey. This was a very lonely time and my walks saved my sanity. Also my girlfriend of the time, Carol, was really good with me and when I had to organise registration and collecting my Dad's things from Hope she was amazing and so kind. We had been going out since my Elective period in 4th year and she had been made ward sister and deservedly so as she was a super nurse.

With none of us being Muslim we had a bit of a dilemma. Although Dad had left no instructions and no will we knew that he would want to be buried according to his beliefs. My Mum contacted an ex-partner of his, a Dr

Choonara from Trafford. We did not really know how to proceed. He reassured my Mum and said that he would attend to everything. The local Mosque, which was very small in those days, soon swung into action and my Dad was buried in a Muslim plot at Peel Green cemetery. We made sure things were done in the way that he would have wanted. The local Muslim clerics told us that women were not usually asked to the graveside but as my Mum and Sister were not Muslim they thought that it would be permissible and they too threw some soil on the coffin. Most months I swing by the cemetery to place some flowers on my Mum and Dad's graves. Although she was not a Muslim my Mum asked to be buried close by my Dad. The Christian practice of allowing more than one to be buried in a grave is not allowed by the Muslims and our Mum is buried just a few feet away.

Carol and I had been going out for a couple of years and although there was nothing seriously wrong I knew that marriage for me was some distance away. I told her that there was nobody else but that I didn't see myself as getting married for the foreseeable future or pushing a pram into Monton. She told me that she'd never asked me to do that. I didn't think it right if I wasted her time even though we were both still in our early twenties! I said I thought we should part. The tricky thing is that we'd booked a two-week holiday to go to Egypt and the Nile and we would both have lost our money if we cancelled. We still went even though it was a difficult time. A short time later we parted and within a couple of weeks after this her Dad died. I telephoned to tell her how sorry I was and reminded her of how good she'd been with me. As is the way with such things loneliness descended and once again it was more of my making than anyone else's.

Just to stop me getting bored a succession of near disasters followed me in my house jobs. There was the time when I took blood from a patient in order to cross-match some blood for the operation that was planned the day after. I phoned the lab so that I could collect the blood and was told that none had been cross-matched for him. I shouted at them as I knew that I had taken the sample myself and even taken it down to the blood bank lab. The technician then told me that they hadn't cross-matched any blood because the sample was labelled with a different name from the accompanying request card. I went down to the lab again to take a fresh sample, having apologised to the patient. My most important apology however was to the chap I'd shouted at. I went to find him so that I could at least do him the courtesy of a face-to-face apology and it taught me a very important lesson – or perhaps I should say several important lessons. When one was tired and strung out it was especially important to try to be patient, tolerant and also aware of one's own failings.

Then there was the time that I was in theatre and the patient was half way through his operation. The consultant anaesthetist said to my consultant that he had better send for the blood that had been cross-matched. I knew there was no blood because I hadn't requested any! I'd asked one of my colleagues and she'd said that a simple group and save was adequate. Mercifully they had this sample and were able to do the cross-match in short order. It was an awkward moment with my just having to admit to my mistake and apologise.

One patient was due to go to theatre. She was found to be a bit anaemic so for 24 hrs before I'd set up an infusion with a slightly wider 'yellow Venflon' which was an intravenous cannula. Through this drip I had run about four units of blood. The venflon was still in when she went down for theatre. The consultant anaesthetist asked me if the drip was still running and I told him that I'd just run all the blood transfusion through it. He decided to inject the anaesthetic drugs through the same venflon. As soon as he started the drip it 'tissued' so that the anaesthetic ran under the skin and not into the circulation. This means discomfort for the patient and also that the anaesthetic won't take until a new drip has been sited. My Registrar told me that the anaesthetist was ranting and raving down in theatre and I'd better get myself down there to apologise. I told him that I'd just run 4 units of blood through it without incident, but thought I'd better do as he suggested and apologise pretty smartish.

Then there was the time that a patient came in for a really big operation. He went down to theatre having been clerked in by me. He was asleep and the surgeon was just checking the notes and discovered that he'd not signed his consent form. This was my job, and a great oversight on my part. The surgeon phoned his wife and asked her if she was happy for him to proceed as the operation was such a large one that, had it been cancelled that day, it would be months before it could be re-arranged.

The saddest thing of all was one day when I was talking to the two cleaners who cleaned the surgical ward. They stopped me and said, "You know, you are the only person who talks to us." I asked them why, that was the case. They told me that most others thought they were too lowly to speak with as they were just cleaners. I told them that their efforts to keep the ward clean were just as important as mine at trying to keep the patients healthy and we were all contributing to the whole. Nobody had a right to look down his nose at another.

Many years later as a young GP I went out to the flats past Barton Aerodrome to see a little baby who was unwell. In those days these flats were really run down and have all been more recently renovated. It was a Sunday afternoon and the family were not my patients. After I'd examined the little girl and sorted her out the father walked me to the door. He told me that they'd seen a lot of doctors. He told me that most didn't give them the time of day because they were poor and lived in a poor part of town. He said that he wanted to thank me for thoroughly examining his daughter and for treating all of them with kindness and respect. I told him that he and his family were no less important to me than any other patient and I was not bothered as to where they lived. If we had no patients then we would not have jobs and he might wish to remind the next doctor that had occasion to visit them of this. I shook his hand and left, feeling both humbled and also complimented.

Coming back to my time as a junior doctor. Mercifully for me, the number of things that went right greatly outnumbered the ones where things had gone wrong and, before I left, the surgeon offered me a glowing reference and was even prepared to speak to a new consultant, if there was a particular job that I was interested in, on my behalf. The same was true for my second housejob in North Wales. Although in this job we worked a 1:3 rota, some friends did an even more demanding one of 1:2 where they were on call alternate weekends and also at least two nights each week.

The poor souls were so tired that they had no time for a social life – or anything other than work!

All in all, I had been very efficient during my house jobs. There was a load of work to do and not a lot of time in which to do it. The houseman was wanted everywhere by everyone. I got into the habit of starting work at 7:30 am. I would then go round and see all my patients. I would have all the blood forms that I needed to take for the following day already filled in and all the bottles labelled. As I did my rounds I would also take the bloods. The bloods would be all set to go for 8:30 am when the consultant or registrar came to assess the patients to look at those recovering, those who could go home and those who needed other things sorting. I would then action any requests from the round. At the same time new patients would start to arrive. These would need clerking in and, ideally, they would need those going home to leave before they could then occupy the same beds and then be examined and clerked in by me. The trouble was that it was often afternoon before the bed was ready and then I could be left with half a dozen patients to clerk in that might take up to an hour each. It would often be too late to get their bloods done. I hit on the idea of using the side-ward and examination room off the ward. I would whisk them in there as soon as the round finished, examine them, write the records up and send their bloods off to the lab. They could then wait for the beds to become available. Then there would be ward work and sometimes, theatre sometimes outpatients and at least two days a week we would be on 'take' where emergency patients would come in. These would need clerking in and all their investigations doing before the senior houseman or registrar came to look at them. Of course in the operative specialties they would often need to go to theatre and sometimes in a hurry. Usually by 6:30pm I was straight, unless of course I was on call, in which case my 'day' was only just beginning. At 6:30pm I would write all the blood requests up for the following day, receive and check all the blood results that had been done that day and then wander home, only for the day to begin again the following morning. It was efficient and it got the job done.

Some of my colleagues emulated my methods in patient management. One of my friends was Eva Jacobs, whom I first met during my elective the previous year. As many of you will know, I met up with her again when we were both GPs at Eccles Health Centre and more latterly at St Andrews. She was also kind enough to edit my first three books and how much she taught me about English! She had been, in a former life, the Head of English at a girls' boarding school. She was houseman to one of the other surgeons. I taught her how to construct her day along efficient lines and she taught me something far more valuable. She'd sit and talk to patients, she'd go off and make them a cup of tea, then she'd sit with them.

Although I wasn't unfriendly with my patients Eva taught me so much about caring for the whole patient – what is known today as holistic care and these wonderful skills that she taught me have been invaluable. It was far more than making the right diagnosis or doing the right tests or putting the right treatment in place and she taught me so much about what, at times, could be missing from this efficient façade.

Many nights a Catholic priest would come on to the wards. He was a wonderful, kind man and devoutly religious. He would offer to see and comfort any of the dying even those who were not practising Catholics, as long as they were prepared to see him. This arrangement worked well and though working all through the night, as well as the day before, and the prospect of the following day to come were tiring there was a calm serenity about the nights and a feeling, as I walked along those still and dark wards and corridors, that we were making a difference.

I remember admitting this chap who was dying with aggressive lung cancer. I clerked him in and his bony, stick-like hand gripped mine. His wasted, sunken eyes stared at me. He told me that he didn't mind what happened that night as long as he felt no pain. I gripped his hand back and promised him that I would do everything in my power to make sure that he was comfortable. Within seconds I'd taken action; I put a drip up and to the drip attached an IVAC which regulated precisely how quickly the drip, and thus any drugs that were in the drip, ran through. I set up a drip of some morphine, something to reduce his anxiety and something to help him forget. Before I left the ward I asked the nurses to call me if he so much as stirred. He went off to sleep. In the early hours of the morning he passed away and they called me. He hadn't woken but the haunted hollowed-out look that he'd had on his face when I admitted him at midnight was now gone and had been replaced by a calmness and a peace in death.

Sadly, it has to be said, not all deaths were calm or peaceful. I remember when I was a medical student; I must have been about twenty-one. A lady was admitted to the Heath hospital. She'd learned that day that her husband had been unfaithful. She'd swallowed one hundred Paracetamol tablets some hours before. She was drifting in and out of consciousness but was also very distressed. We were desperately trying to transfer her across the city to Cardiff Royal Infirmary so that she could be dialysed. Sadly, she died as we were transferring her into the Ambulance. The poor soul had a dreadful death. I learned too, that she had two small children.

In my Paediatric block, which was just before I qualified, we admitted a teenager who was about 15. She'd been unlucky in catching chickenpox. Normally such cases are pretty mild and given time will resolve on their own. Sadly the thing that brought her to the brink of death and gave her life-changing scarring that day was a calamitous and negligent mistake by her GP who for some reason put her on oral steroids. Under such influence the chickenpox virus becomes very aggressive and she was plunged into extreme ill health with vast areas of blackened, blood filled blisters all over her body. To be honest, I do not know if she survived. Our Registrar was so upset, he got us out of there pretty quickly and kept asking what had prompted her GP to do such a thing. We all make mistakes and sometimes it's there but for the grace of God. I sometimes see this poor girl in my most terrifying of nightmares.

Another case seared into my mind, was the young woman, when I was working in Casualty, who came in having taken an overdose, after feeling depressed, of her mother's tablets. In those days the Tricyclic antidepressants were in widespread use. These were effective but, in overdose, they were really nasty customers and a really dreadful death was about to be visited on this poor young girl. We tried absolutely everything to protect her heart from the arrhythmia the tablets caused and her breathing as she'd vomited and aspirated. We tried repeatedly to stabilise her in order to transfer her to Intensive Care. The doctor from there came down later to thank us all for our efforts but she'd died some hours later. The whole department was in shock; a couple of the nurses were in tears.

Then there was a baby that had been brought into Casualty, unwell, by her parents. I examined the baby and did all the tests, all of which were normal. I just wasn't happy with her, however, and decided to phone the Paediatrician to admit her overnight. He told me via the telephone that I had done all the tests that he would have done and I should discharge the baby. I did this and went off shift. In the middle of the night the baby was brought back, now moribund, and spent the next 10 days in Intensive care. I was dreading the baby dying as of course the Paediatrician had not written anything in the notes and the blame was all mine. I spent those days full of dread, which was surely only what I deserved. The spoken word can be a fleeting and erratic thing. Mercifully, the baby recovered and went home. I learnt a very powerful lesson there and then; not only that, a bit like at school, some could be trusted and some could not, but also that if anyone suggested a certain line of management I would insist that they come to the department and write in the notes. This made sure that they bore responsibility, rather than being able to hide behind another, after some verbal exchange that was not recorded.

I often think of these patients. I wonder if I will see them again the day I die. If they were still able to talk to me I know that they'd ask me if I had always tried to do my best for each and every one of them without fear or favour. I would like to be able to look them all in the eye and tell them that this was so.

Sometimes, without doubt, my deliverance was due to others. I remember a young woman coming in to Casualty in

North Wales having taken an overdose of tablets. In those days we'd do blood tests and, more often than not, wash out their stomachs. You will remember that I had had this done as a baby but mercifully did not remember it. This young woman was pleading with me that she had not taken as many tablets as she first indicated and did not want the tube passing into her stomach. I was about to believe her and rely simply on the bloods, which could be a dangerous assumption to make. The sister who was with me grabbed the tube and inserted it into her stomach to perform the washout with the words,

"You are a good doctor, I can't have you blowing your career on this scum!" The young woman went home the following day, no doubt chastened by her experience, and I had been given one or two important lessons too.

My house job in North Wales was hectic not only because of the rota, but also because my immediate superior liked to stay in bed all evening and would not get up to help me. I remember he was lucky to have a stunning wife! This meant that I was very much on my own and would take all the calls from GPs wanting to admit patients. Doctors would often split this so that both could get a little sleep. Sometimes in summer it could take hours for patients to arrive after having take the call. I would then have to see them and sort them out. My Registrar was technically available but the chain of command was that I should phone my SHO. I remember struggling all through the night with this still quite young woman who had crashing heart failure. In those days we had very few drugs that would help with heart failure; how different things are now. I struggled and struggled all through the night. I phoned my SHO who, from his bed, told me that I had done everything and could not suggest anything further. She died in the early hours of the morning and I felt really desolate and very tired.

My registrar who was my SHO's immediate superior sensed my difficulties. He told me that it had been noted that I was bearing much of the work burden and the consultant had made a note of it. When the time came to leave I was given a glowing reference that assisted me in applying for my next jobs. I am not sure if my SHO received a similar reference.

Without doubt, seeing patients get better and go home was by far the most rewarding of outcomes. Watching people deteriorate was never easy, but this scenario can often tax a doctor's professional and emotional skill to its maximum. Many of the hill farmers could speak no English and I would, under such circumstances, ask one of the nurses on the ward to act as interpreter. Such folk were very warm, gentle people who seemed grateful for the help and medical care that came their way.

As you might expect, I was lonely again and with my Dad just having died it was a difficult time. Long walks on deserted beaches helped and it was also made more enjoyable by the warm spring and expanding days of summer. I would drive a bit further each night that I wasn't on call and then find a quiet beach or footpath to walk and then return to my little room that was just off one of the medical wards.

I had done one of my attachments as a medical student in Llandudno and one in Bodelwyddan. In Lllandudno I had met a really nice person, Gaynor. She was the houseman and thus a year or two older than I was. We became good friends though I could never quite manage to tell her how besotted I was with her. The nice thing is that the poor soul worked a 1 in 2 and would be ferociously busy; I would be happy to help her in whatever way I could. I got to Llandudno General very early one morning; she had 5 patients to clerk, had had about an hour's sleep and was busy clerking a patient, looking very tired with her nightie tucked into her jeans! Mercifully, my expanding skill set meant I was able to be of help to her with a lot of the routine stuff, including the forms and taking and sending all the bloods that she needed doing. Although this was not particularly professionally demanding, it did take a lot of time and it helped her enormously.

A year or so later, when I was qualified, she was doing her GP training rotation locally and we met up again. Her parents had a holiday cottage in Penmaenmawr. One night I drove out to visit her from my base at the C&A. They were building the A55 and a long, long section was single file and controlled by a set of lights that took an age to change. On my way back to the hospital it had gone dark and I assumed that the roadworks had been sent another way. I did not realise that the traffic lights had been blown over by the developing storm, and I shot through. After some considerable distance I met a chap really hurtling the opposite way who had presumably come through on a green light. Just in time we both managed to brake and I managed to swerve around him by actually passing my little Metro through the coned-off section and miraculously was able to get back on the road with no other cars coming. He was not very pleased and it was a bit of a lucky escape for us as we could have both been killed in that stormy night.

When I got to Gaynor's she asked me if I fancied a take away and off we went in her little white sports car and drove to Conwy where at that time there was an Indian restaurant.

We ordered the curry and a few minutes later they stacked it all in a tall brown paper bag. We left after paying and ventured out into the storm-torn night. Within minutes of our leaving the restaurant the bag became soaked through; the whole thing promptly burst and the entire stack of curry was deposited on the pavement and, without further ado, washed away in the storm. We went back to the restaurant and Gaynor explained what had happened and could we order another lot of curry, please. The power of a pretty girl was very much in evidence that night. They promptly presented us with a fresh lot and refused any payment. The Indian restaurant is not there these days but I think of it whenever I journey to North Wales, and Conwy in particular.

The other advantage of working in the more peripheral hospitals was that the students and doctors got to do lots and lots of procedures. I routinely inserted chest drains, performed liver and kidney biopsies and lumbar punctures right on the ward. I think these days no junior doctor would be allowed to do these things, or if so, they would only be done in theatre. I remember one day inserting a chest drain into a 12 year-old boy who had come in with a pneumothorax, where one of his lungs had gone down. I asked not to do it but my Registrar was insistent and said that the difficult ones were the only way to really learn. I froze the spot between his ribs where the spike would go through, and this was on the middle of the ward, with the local anaesthetic, cut the outer muscle of the chest wall with a sharp scalpel and did my best to stop his staring at the trocar as I pushed on the end of it. This long trocar, which is like a foot-long spike with a tube around it was just entering his lung. Suddenly, he cried out and rotated sideways. I thought for sure the trocar would pierce his heart or his aorta and he would promptly expire on the spot, leaving me with a lifetime of guilt and regret. Mercifully, this did not happen and a couple of days later I, a very relieved junior doctor, saw him walk out of the hospital for home with his mum and dad.

Though the hours were incredibly long and the workload followed suit, there was something about that time in the stillness of the middle of the night. I would perhaps be in quiet conversation with the night nursing team, by the little lights that would blink from the syringe drivers and monitors and pumps, or even walking along the deserted corridors. It was often a time for reflection and deep thought about what was important and what wasn't and although I could not work at that pace today, I was glad that I did it, if only because it taught me a lot about myself. Indeed there was, most nights, but not all, a magical time. This invariably arose when I was alone, perhaps walking to the wards from the on-call room or I was moving from ward to ward. This existed, as the song says, between the dark and the light. Life and death would stalk the wards. Among the mayhem and the extreme work and the all-sapping tiredness would stand a calm, a sense of duty and a devotion to one's patient and one's profession. One's determination to use absolutely everything at one's disposal to save a life, or at the very least to make sure that nobody died in pain, was uppermost in the vast majority of young doctors' minds. The fact that we'd usually seen them be admitted in the day and then be able to follow their progress for good or ill right through the night gave each and every one of us a unique knowledge and insight of that interface between death or life and success or failure. The Catholic priest understood this and he had obviously found his calling at such times. This too, on a slightly different but complementary plane, was where we found ours. Occasionally the priest would ask me if I could do anything for Mr 'So and So' in bed 6 and I would shake my head and say that sadly the time had come for his ministrations rather than mine. I wonder if the more sparing shift system as worked by junior doctors today still allows for this wonderful time that I was glad and honoured to have experienced.

Although patients passing away was hard to handle, as long as I knew that I had done my utmost then there was at least a sense of having fought with every ounce of resource and skill at my disposal. As I said above, before I die I will see these patients again and I suspect they will ask me if I did my best at all times despite tiredness and sometimes difficulties, raising my game in the middle of the night. I'd like to feel I could do this with each and every one of them.

The thing that was even harder than this, however, was the time when I was was seconded to one of the Consultant Haematologists. There would be about half a dozen patients who would present for day-case drips containing chemotherapy. In those days it was pretty toxic stuff. It would take an hour just to draw up, mix and check, and then an hour to give. Much of it would strip varnish from a table if it were spilled. It would be essential to wear goggles or eye protection as a little splash in one's eye would be very painful. One patient read her notes after the nurse had left them on the table waiting for the consultant to come in. She discovered that her prognosis was poor. She got up, said that she was leaving the hospital and would refuse all further treatment. I think she took the view that there was simply no point in going through the stresses and pain of chemotherapy if there wasn't a good chance of coming through the other side.

Even worse than this, is that they would associate the side effects that they would get, such as marked vomiting, with my face. The poor souls would start vomiting as soon as they entered the ward or, worse still, as soon as they set eyes on me. This was the hardest time of my life as it seemed to erase and go against everything that I was trying to do for these unfortunate people – to get them better not make them feel dreadful. Mercifully, this did not go on for long as, after a few weeks, the Haematologist got his own houseman and presumably he or she did all the drips and the administering of chemotherapy.

I was planning to set up home in Wales as I would often walk round Beaumaris or Newborough sands in the evenings. My mum was on her own after my Dad's death. The consultant warned me about bringing my mum to live with me in Wales as, in his opinion, she'd be out of her comfort zone and would miss friends of her own that would allow her to reconnect with her life. I was able to go home most weekends that I wasn't on call and the drive along the A55 that was being developed was always interesting.

It was also true that working such long hours and going home at weekends meant that there wasn't much time for loneliness. I saw Gaynor occasionally but she was busy with her GP rotation where different jobs would be taken on in a 3-year rotation before one could apply to become a GP. I was always terrified of letting slip just what I thought about her and that this would instantly mean the end of our friendship. Of course, if one were bold, there were lots of pretty girls on the wards to ask out. This didn't seem right if I was planning to move back to England. I remember the time I was a student I did my Obstetric and Paediatric attachment in Bangor. In order to complete the module each medical student needed to conduct twenty deliveries. The unit was full of qualified midwives many of whom came from Ireland. They were stunning girls and also quite lonely. They had the jet-black hair with the fair skin and would often have blue or mesmerising green eyes. It was very tempting to ask one out as many of my contempories did. I considered that at that time I had a girlfriend at home and, although she might never find out, I would know and I wouldn't have liked it if she'd done that to me. This was quite a good defence against the wonderful midwives' undoubted charms!

Although I was unlucky in North Wales, with my immediate superior, my SHO, wishing to stay in bed each night and not help out in any way, this was emphatically not the case at Hope Hospital. My SHO there, Nigel Scott was amazing and helped so much at all levels. He was so hard working and so impressive. It was an absolute pleasure to work alongside such a dedicated person and I was not at all surprised some years later when he became a consultant surgeon at Hope. As a GP I would often refer patients to him. Some years' later he moved to Preston in order to head up the surgical unit there. I heard that he's recently retired. I never did hear what happened to my SHO from North Wales. I wonder if he learned much about either medicine, or himself, by choosing to stay in bed while I did his work as well as mine.

One of my friends was in a very busy job and after a particularly busy night where he'd had no sleep at all he realised he still had five patients to clerk who'd been admitted. He asked his SHO if he could see one or two for him. The SHO smiled and said, "Dear boy, you realise that s*it rolls downhill and you, sadly, are right at the bottom. Goodnight."

My next job was as an SHO in Rochdale casualty. Although this unit did not take accident casualties off the motorway, Death Valley, it was still a really busy unit. What's more you learnt stuff very quickly or you were in danger of sending the wrong patient home. I used to hear tales of how many SHOs had been required to come back to the unit years after they'd departed because of some horrible misdiagnosis that had occurred on their watch.

So many cases and presentations impact on me to this day. Like the little old lady that went walking in Rochdale for some shopping. They'd fitted some new windows in the block of flats she walked past. One of these windows detached and a pane of glass hit her on the head, from thirty feet up, but did not kill her, at least not straight away. Another injury that impacted on me was the truck driver that jumped out of his cab. His wedding ring got stuck on the cab side as he dropped down and de-gloved his finger. This means that only the bone is left as the ring scrapes off all the flesh as he drops down. I had never seen this before, but the Consultant knew exactly what he'd done and how. The only treatment is to amputate the finger. It left such an impression on me that when I got married I asked Frankie, my wife, if she would mind if I didn't wear a wedding ring. Even to this day I shudder when I think of that poor man's finger being traumatised in this way.

We also had our fair share of drunks and overdoses and self inflicted harm. We worked more of a definite shift pattern as there was little chance of getting any rest when on duty. One morning about 7 am I was on the unit and my shift was due to finish at 8 am. It had been quiet through the night and I was looking forward to getting home. Suddenly loads of ambulances turned up following a house fire and about 10 – 20 people came in, all with smoke inhalation. That was a very long and very busy hour and I was very pleased to see my colleagues who came on shift at 8!

I was working with five lads all of whom were Scottish apart from one chap from Manchester. They asked me if I would like Christmas off in return for covering them all while they went to Scotland for New Year. I had about four days off over Christmas, but then of course had to cover them. I worked a solid 48 hours over New Year with only one colleague appearing on one of the day shifts; otherwise I was working continuously without a break. Despite it being very tiring, it was a fair swap and I had no regrets about doing it, although once again I was delighted to see them return.

I remember the Christmas party and at its end I was planning to drive home. Being on my own again I'd offered a lift to one of the nurses on the unit who was really pretty and whom I'd been dying to get to know a little more. Anyway, here she was in my car. One of the more senior nursing staff asked me if she could have a lift home. I agreed straight away. She was a nice person and a really good nurse. She was a year or two older than me, maybe late 20s. I'd had my 25th Birthday while working in Casualty and one of the nurses announced with delight that she'd found a grey hair on my head. In those days I had wonderful thick black hair that I really miss!

As we got to the nurse's house, I stopped the car, and she started crying. She told me that her husband always punished her if she went on any nights out without him. She told me that she would be locked out at least until morning. She would either have to knock on a neighbour's door or failing this would have to sleep in their shed. I must stress that she'd behaved at the party impeccably and was not in any way indecorous or drunk. I was aghast that a grown man could treat his wife this way for having the temerity to simply go on a work's do. She became really upset and I asked her if I could drop her anywhere else with friends or relatives. I thought about taking her home and knew that my mum would find a bed for her, but what came next chilled me to the core. She told me that if she went somewhere else, even to a female friend, his anger would know no bounds and she would be made to suffer for weeks to come. Her only course of action now was for her to beg on her own doorstep, so that he would know she was there. He, of course, would not let her in and she'd end up in the shed or next door until morning. I was going to suggest that she phone the police but in those days they did not interfere even when a poor decent woman who had done nothing wrong was abused in this way. It made me feel so sad leaving my colleague in this way after midnight but she assured me that if I got involved I would be dragged in too. I felt so disturbed that I suggested to the pretty girl, who was still in the back of my car and who I had been dying to spend a little free time with, that I took her back to her residence. To this day I am amazed at the physical and emotional hurt that so-called or previously devoted couples can exact on one another.

Domestic disputes notwithstanding, my time in A&E was wonderful and I think if I hadn't chosen General Practice, then I'd have done Casualty. I also received another really good reference from the A&E consultant. He told me that I could write my own reference and that he'd sign it. I didn't dare! The reference he did provide stood me in good stead for my next job, Elderly Care medicine. This was a job that ran for 12 months and extended across the old Ladywell hospital before they pulled it down and made it into West One shopping centre. Part of the rotation was also via the professorial unit at Hope Hospital. At Ladywell my Registrar was a wonderful Indian chap called Srinivas. He spoke with a delightful far back accent. One night on-call a GP phoned him looking for a bed for an elderly patient who needed admission. Srinivas took the call and said, "I am frightfully sorry old chap but we're absolutely chokkers!" Although elderly care was not regarded as being a particularly salubrious job, it taught me so much about disease and also handling frail patients.

However, one incident nearly caused me to resign from the job and leave medicine. I was on call for the weekend and the Consultant warned me to be on my toes as they were closing one of the wards for maintenance and moving the entire ward full of patients into a temporary ward while the work was done. I remember he told me that elderly patients could be fragile and simply the act of moving them could upset them and throw them off balance. I must confess that I did not believe him. Most of the patients were simply moved by a couple of porters and never left their beds. How wrong I was! I think there were fifteen deaths that weekend. Everywhere I looked there was a death. One poor lady came in simply so that her relatives could have a holiday. She passed away within 24 hours of her being admitted. I have neither before nor since seen so many patients who all 'went off', as doctors say, at the same time. I was in a state of shock and spent much of the weekend working with my

Registrar who mercifully was very much a hands-on chap who shared the burden with me. I was devastated come the Monday morning and I remember seeing all the notes in a row of all the patients who'd succumbed. I thought for sure that medicine could not possibly be for me and that I'd better hand in my notice and leave and do something else. I can't really remember what or who changed my mind. I do remember having long discussions with my Registrar.

Anyway, for whatever reason, I decided to hang in and things suddenly started to improve. A couple of weeks later a chap was admitted who rapidly became confused and then paranoid. He barricaded himself in the side ward and threatened to set the whole place on fire. In order to subdue a patient quickly, in those days, we'd use a syringe of paraldehyde. This would work quickly and safely but would sting a bit. The problem was that as soon as it was drawn up into a plastic syringe it would start to melt the syringe. One therefore did not have much time. Glass syringes were pretty rare and I doubt that one would find them at all these days though I do have one or two that belonged to my Dad. So, there I was, little me, the side ward had glazed panels and the patient got more agitated as soon as he saw us approaching. We crouched down below the half-height panels, I was clutching the syringe of paraldehyde and behind me were two porters and behind them was the hospital administrator! Mercifully, I did not have to use the syringe in anger. I was able to get in there and talk to the patient. He calmed down quite a bit and the immediate threat was over. We managed to identify the source of his acute confusion, usually infection, and upon our treating this he improved nicely. Occasionally patients would get violent and sometimes we'd have to get porters in to help us calm them down. Mercifully this was rare and being a small chap it struck me that if I did not them antagonise even an agitated patient they would see that I was no threat to them and hopefully cool down. I'll tell you later about the time that a patient trapped me in my room and refused to let me out.

Once again I was lucky to get super references and also made the acquaintance of some wonderful doctors. There was always the odd one who would let you down. I remember one of the doctors at Hope; if he'd seen an elderly patient he would simply write on the Casualty card, 'Looks like a stroke, refer Geriatrics'. This was all he would do. Many, many others would examine the patient, do the bloods and write a detailed report. This would save a lot of time when one was in a hurry. As always, however, it revealed those whom one could trust and rely on and those who one could not.

I then moved on to Obstetrics and Gynaecology at Hope. This was a relentless job. We were busy through the day and also really busy at night. Nights on call would mean little sleep and this would also extend through the weekends. Mercifully, the more senior medical staff were amazing as were the nurses on the Gynaecology wards and, without doubt, the midwives. We also would be required to do a clinic in outpatients and also a theatre list for minor procedures such as D&Cs. I'd hooked up with Gaynor, my friend from N Wales, and she'd started as a GP in South Manchester. Once or twice a week I'd journey to the pubs and restaurants of Disley, Hattersley and other places I'd not been to before. I'd also not plucked up the courage to tell her that I was, still, besotted by her though I did persuade her on one occasion to come and say "Hello" to my Mum.

Whenever I did my outpatient clinic one of the more senior midwives, Lorraine, would assist me. This was unusual as the senior staff usually went in with the Registrar. In any event we struck up a friendship and I would talk about my friend Gaynor and she would talk about her fiancé who was back in the North East where she was from. She was an amazing midwife and, by common consent, the darling of the unit. She was the cleverest, the most superb and the prettiest girl in the whole unit.

One day Gaynor took me to one side and told me that she'd been contacted out of the blue by an old flame with whom she wanted to rekindle their relationship. I must say, though it was an unusual thing for me to be dumped, this was the nicest way in which to do it and of course she only went up in my estimation. We still wrote to each other but otherwise it was over. The song that reminds me of this time is "Ocean Deep" by Cliff Richard, it was one of Gaynor's favourites. It seemed that Lorraine's relationship had also ended and we were to be found counselling each other between patients that we'd see in the outpatient clinics.

One weekend I was on call; I was walking along the corridor to the maternity block. Lorraine was at the end of her shift and was leaving. She stopped me in the corridor and asked me if she could have a word with me. She told me that she was very sorry to put this on me but she couldn't stop thinking about me and she just had to tell me. It's important to realise that not only was Lorraine the best midwife on the unit but she was also the prettiest. I'd been very fortunate with my girlfriends for someone who wasn't particularly tall, exciting or handsome; I'd been out with some super girls and considered myself a lucky chap.

I remember one of my friends who was a stunning, tall model went to a fancy dress party as the Martini Girl, complete with roller blades and short skater skirt! I wasn't at the party, sadly, but I bet it was an exciting place to be – especially when she showed up. Whenever we went out and she sported heels, she would tower over me. I was more excited by this than perturbed and I cannot see why short men have a problem with it. I just counted myself as being fortunate.

Coming back to Lorraine, I told her that I was very, very flattered. In those days it was unusual for girls to ask boys out and I don't think she was seeking this. I think she just wanted to tell me how she felt. I was gobsmacked, as they say. I was still pining after Gaynor and my usual strategy at such times was simply to work through it and, a few weeks down the line, maybe try to find another relationship. I knew that I'd rather be lonely than use someone to fill my loneliness. Being stopped in this way left me unusually speechless. We talked for a little while and I asked Lorraine if perhaps we could go out for a drink some time and talk some more. A short time later we started dating and once again I was very fortunate to be in her company and also working with her and her colleagues on a professional level who were excellent.

Weekends were especially busy. Once again I would try to start really early and I would immediately go round the Gynaecology wards with the sister in charge. She would discuss with me all the cases she was happy with and, also, the ones she was more worried about. I would then present a report to the Registrar who normally would have to do this. It saved a lot of his time and also meant he could concentrate on areas like the patients we were worried about, the emergency admissions and also the labour ward, where things could go off precipitously.

One night I admitted this poor lady who, I believed, was having her second tubal pregnancy. She'd already lost a tube from the previous one. I was really worried about her as I thought she was bleeding internally. I phoned my Reg to say that I was prepping her for theatre and to ask that he join me as soon as possible. He told me that he was on the labour ward and about to do a low forceps delivery. He would be about half an hour. I told him that I didn't think she had this time and perhaps he could go straight to theatre and I would go and do the forceps. Mercifully, he trusted my assessment without further ado. He went straight to theatre just as the patient was going under the anaesthetic. He took over two litres of blood from her abdominal cavity and if we had not swapped round in this way the poor lady would have succumbed.

Worse than the medical emergencies were the pickles that occasionally we found ourselves in the middle of. I was on call with Dave, my Registrar, all weekend. He was a superb Obstetrician and a delight to work with. We were doing an emergency section in theatre. One of the midwives who was working in the community had been allowed into theatre as part of her refresher training. Just as soon as the baby came out, suddenly this pair of gloved hands came forward to grab the baby. Sadly, she had not gowned up, which meant that her arms were not sterile. She had broken the sterile field. Dave stood there really angry and upset. Things for that moment seemed completely paralysed as he could not believe what had happened. He shouted at her that she had broken his sterile field. I kept saying to him, "Come on, Dave, let's just close up."

The midwives said that he should not shout in that way as she had not been trained properly. Sadly the two sides broke apart and an uncooperative atmosphere prevailed all weekend with each side not really talking to the other. The lady and the baby were fine. We kept her in for an extra 24 hours and she was fully informed as to what had happened but she and the baby escaped without incident. Sadly, all weekend I was plunged into doing my best to work as a go-between from the medical team to the midwives. In an acute unit this was very difficult. I am not sure if it was late that night or the early hours of the following day but I chanced upon what can only be a high-risk strategy. I've often been blessed with having good ideas in tight spots; sometimes they can be a bit wacky and sometimes can go badly awry but in the event I decided to go with it. I told the midwives that Dave wanted to apologise. At the same time I went to find Dave to tell him that the midwives wanted to apologise. He came on the unit with a face like thunder, then broke into a smile and hugged the senior midwife and head of the unit. The crisis was over and normal service was resumed.

Weeks and weeks later, the day I left this job he took me to one side and said to me, "The midwives, didn't really apologise did they?" I told him that it had been an absolute pleasure working with him and sometimes an SHO had to do what was needed for the greater good. He shook my hand.

One other crisis shocked me and that concerned a poor lady who was pregnant and who had an active herpes infection. Under such circumstances it is necessary to deliver the patient by section because if the baby becomes infected with herpes it can be lethal. There are no other special precautions; the risk is purely to the baby at delivery.

Unfortunately the poor lady was imprisoned in a solitary room. She was having full barrier nursing, where the nurses would gown up with mask, aprons and gloves before they went in. She was not allowed out and was becoming distressed. I waited for the infection control nurse to come, thinking a little common sense would prevail. Unfortunately she redoubled the precautions, even though there was no risk to anyone else. The poor lady told me, choking back the tears, that she was really upset. She said that they were bringing all her meals on paper plates and she wouldn't mind but they were bringing her hot drinks in cups and saucers. What she didn't know is that they were breaking these and throwing them as soon as she'd finished with them. She wasn't in labour and her baby was fine, so I suggested that she simply go home and she could always return for a booked section nearer term. This worked well and the poor lady got to go home. It was a sign of how a little knowledge could get whipped up into near mass panic.

Chapter XI

General Practice

I then started my GP trainee year. Some time before, a local GP who had taken over my Dad's practice at Eccles Health Centre when he retired visited my mum. He asked me if I was planning to become a GP and if so would I like to do my trainee year with him. I accepted. He was a bitter and spiteful man who simply could not forgive the local hospital for passing him over when he was a registrar in surgery and giving the job to someone else. In point of fact the surgeon who was appointed was superb and a brilliant surgeon. My GP Trainer, the then Registrar, immediately left and became a GP but unfortunately never forgot what he perceived were the injustices done to him, which he assumed were down to his colour. This was a shame as he had a clever and agile mind and was a very good and successful GP. He was a good businessman. At all stages, however, his bitterness came to the fore. He simply could not forgive my Dad for being the mild-mannered and emollient person that he was. I remember the day he came to visit my Mum. My Dad had retired and, talking about him when he was in the same room, he said, "Oh don't worry about him, ignore him, he is just an old man." I think rather than accepting the job that he offered I should have taken him to one side and asked him not to talk to my father in that way. More than this, the trainee was simply a skivvy who did all the trainer's work and also the work of the trainer's wife who had a list of her own and whom we never saw. The trainee was expected to do all the trainer's on-call as well as running a full surgery and all the wife's on-call. Many years later one of the receptionists reported this practice and although I was a local GP at the time I never learned what the result of this had been.

He would often rant and rave at how soft my Dad had been. Typical words would be, "I'm not like your Dad; I will fight these people (his GP colleagues) if they try to beat me. I will take a shop in Eccles if I have to and take all their patients." His other party piece was dealing with those who dared to call him out at night. This was unusual, as I would be doing all his on-call anyway! In any event he would often say, "If they call me out I will send them on the bus to town (to the all-night chemist) for a prescription of acetylsalicylic acid (common aspirin) and insist they need to start it that night." This was their 'punishment' for daring to trouble him.

I remember one day my receptionist, who was a young woman called Hilary, was sitting in the office. The office had a wall of glass louvres that then pointed into the waiting room. She had her back to the waiting room and was eating a yoghurt, it being a quiet lunchtime, while sitting on the desk that faced the waiting room. My trainer came in and there were two patients in the waiting room, one of whom was a little old lady. The trainer asked Hilary, "Who is that Bengali man in the waiting room?" She turned round and scanned the waiting room. She turned back and, without blinking, said to my trainer, "Who do you mean, Doctor?"

Hilary was an amazing receptionist. I remember the winter that Dr Lindsay caught glandular fever. It was our busiest time. Hilary and I ran the whole practice for six weeks while he was off and I really couldn't have done it without her. In my time I also had other amazing receptionists like Shelley, Linda, Margo, Roddy, Lawrence and so many others who I just could not have coped without. More recently, at St Andrews although I no longer have my own personal receptionists they are all absolutely amazing and work so hard, often with little recognition. They have all worked so hard and have unfailingly been patient and kind. I certainly couldn't have done my job without them.

I remember, too, that I still had an interest in electronics. I'd seen a circuit for a simple light chaser. This was basically four tiny LED lights that ran in a sequence. I uprated all the components, including the driving transistors, through which all the power would be switched. I mounted the whole thing in a water-proof box and then connected the circuit board through a water-proof socket and cable to a much larger sequence of sixteen rectangular yellow LEDs. These were then mounted below the radiator on my car to make a 'Knight Rider' sequence of 'running lights'. One patient saw me drive up to his house. He saw the little lights flash in sequence. It was a foggy day. He met me at the door and said, "Doctor, I see those lights that run under your radiator; I can see they are there to help you align your car with the pavement." I thanked him profusely and humbly for thinking such thoughts about me but had to tell him they were simply for show, and didn't really serve a useful purpose other than a bit of fun. He looked very puzzled!

Once again I would handle all the nights on call on my own. If I got really stuck my trainer would issue wise words from his house, which was 10 miles away, but never offer to come to my assistance. I learnt quickly.

The year was soon over and I was accepted by a partnership in Lowton, just outside Leigh. This partnership of two women doctors took me on as their list was growing steadily. Each week there would be twenty or thirty medical cards on my desk of patients who wanted to register. The place was so busy that we had two surgeries, a main surgery and a branch. The idea was to build a new larger surgery somewhere between them. I remember one chap came to see me in his Ferrari, which he parked just in front of our surgery on Slag Lane; it stopped all the traffic. The other point is that there was a lot of building in Lowton and lots of young families, as well as more senior ones at the Golbourne end of the practice area where there were still a lot of miners. I was planning to buy a house in Lowton or Culcheth and move there. For the time being I was still driving from my mum's house in Monton, just next door to the house I was born in on Monton Green.

Then, tragically, in October 1986 Dr Borkin came back off holiday and, without warning, died. This was a very sad state of affairs. He was such a lovely man and so well liked by his patients. Soon after Dr Lindsay approached me to see if I would join him and move from Lowton. My partners in Lowton were very upset that I should want to leave. Much of their future strategy was built around my staying and also taking part in the building of a surgery. These plans would have to be put on hold if I left and in addition the area was considerable under-doctored, which of course is why we were so busy. Neither the doctors nor the staff could quite forgive me for wanting to move back to Eccles.

I would continue to pop back at weekends to visit one or two ex-patients purely on a social level. One such patient, Walter Potter, had just lost his wife. He was so upset, having lost her, that I used to pop and see him even when he moved into a nursing home. He told me that he used to be a projectionist at Golbourne cinema. This was an unusual thing as I knew he could neither read nor write. I asked him how he knew which film he was about to screen if he could not read. He told me that he would simply place his hand on the can of film and he would 'sense' whether it was the correct one or not. He told me that he'd only made one mistake in 20 years!

Moving back to Eccles Health Centre, however, was a good move, just a mile from home and the place where, briefly, my Dad worked. It seemed like coming home.

I blitzed my new room and had it decorated. My Mum and sister bought me a new leather desk set from M&S and I had all my certificates framed including the latest one the MRCGP, which is the Royal College of Gen Practitioners. This exam I took in Edinburgh as I wanted to see where my Dad had studied.

Well, the exam was going really badly. Just about every question they asked me I fumbled for the answer. Suddenly the examiner noticed my tie. My Dad was sent, before he died, a 400th year commemorative tie of Edinburgh University. The examiner homed in on this, "Ah, that's a very nice tie you have on there, Dr Behardien." I told the examiner that it was my Dad's and he'd been a graduate of Edinburgh. It was as though someone rang a bell and I switched in that instance from not answering any questions to answering them all. It was like one of these magic spells one sees in adventure movies. Whatever question was asked of me, I suddenly knew the answer. I sailed through and passed my MRCGP easily.

I remember when I was a little boy, though never my favourite, unlike Thunderbirds and Captain Scarlet, Joe 90 was on. In this programme, for those of you who are too young to remember, this little boy had his brain programmed so that he could become an expert in anything just by putting his special glasses on. I am sure one or two more recent films have copied this plot line, in the same way as The Avengers (the Hollywood one, not the Patrick Macnee one!) have copied the flying aircraft carrier, Cloudbase, from Captain Scarlet. This is where the Angels flew from of course in case any of you need your memory jogging.

Things settled down very nicely at Eccles Health Centre and I was working with a group of honest, straightforward and kind GPs who were a pleasure to work with. The trouble was the building was growing too small for our needs. My secretary would come down after surgery and would take dictation in short-hand. She would then type up the letters. The letters would be then ready for signing. One day I bought an Amstrad 1640 personal computer, complete with a dot matrix printer. Overnight the secretaries threw away their typewriters and we had started word processing! I was not quite finished, however. I came across a database program that would run on a PC, DataEase. I used this to programme a complete suite of databases for use in General Practice. Using this we could keep our entire Age Sex Register, Patient summaries, visit records, smear records and so on. Most significantly we could run reports of how many patients we'd seen in a month, how many were due smears and injections and so on. Of course this seems absolutely routine these days but at that time it was all pretty new and groundbreaking. We'd bought a computer which had a 'data pac'. This meant that the 30Mbyte hard drive could be ejected. This contained all the data and thus even when one was stolen no patient data could be accessed. Dr Broxton called it a 'loaf of bread'. We started printing summaries of our electronic records to accompany our word processed letters when a patient was admitted or referred to hospital. To begin with this was used just by me and my patients. Within a few weeks, however, the other doctors asked me if they could also use it. They bought their own computer complete with 'loaf of bread' and started doing what I was doing. I copied the program and added all their patients. A little later on we installed a Novell network and linked computers on each doctor's desk. The network cable then went right round the building and into the secretaries' room. When it rained there would be a glitch in the wire and we'd have to terminate the network at the end doctor's desk so that we could all still use it.

My program went from strength to strength. So many came to look at it and liked it. A few of us formed Practease. This was one of the first computer programs for business to use full colour. There was a demonstration facility at the FHSA (Family Health Services Authority) in Bolton. They had all the computer programs on display and we applied to have ours on demonstration. Some days later I went up there as a secret shopper and the girls doing the demonstrations told me, without knowing that I was 'Practease', that it was the most popular. We marketed it nationally and an advert went out in one of the GP newspapers. I remember the day that the phone line was connected and it started ringing and didn't stop. Orders came in from up and down the country. I was working as a GP one day and the next I'd be in South Wales demonstrating.

Sadly, we were phoned by the head of the demonstration in Bolton whom we found out later had been discharged from the Army in suspicious circumstances. He told me that our program was the most popular and he foresaw a bright future for it. He was prepared to recommend it, but he was expecting kickbacks for doing so. I explained to him (I believe he later went to jail) that we could not do business in this way. It was either worthy of recommendation on its own merits or it was not. This was a sad reflection and a sharp lesson of how some people transact business. It brought it home to me that for all its faults the NHS and the care it provides were never dependent on how much money someone had paid or how wealthy someone was. Worse was to come. We went in with another company who could assist us on a national scale. We had six cars on the road, 4 demonstrators and full-time support staff and secretarial staff. The bills were enormous. Though the sales kept coming in the overheads were going up even faster. It was a very exciting time but also accompanied by ferocious worries. Eventually we just had to pull the plug and found a company that could take over all our sites. The fascinating thing is that in those days our standard fileserver had a disc capacity of 20Mbytes. If the customer paid extra they could have a Compaq fileserver that had a disc of 40Mbytes! Interesting times, and though I suspect if we had been a bit more savvy and also a bit less green we could have made a go of it, it was perhaps all for the best when we wound it up.

Back at work, I suggested that we apply to go Fundholding and this was the most successful time in General Practice, simply because the money followed the patient. It meant more work on our part but it also meant we could secure great services for all our patients, and also very quickly. We used to negotiate amazing contracts on behalf of our patients with local hospitals. Any savings from these negotiations could be ploughed back into patient care thus allowing us to expand the range of treatments we could get for them. For instance we were allowed to refer six patients a year for private varicose vein treatment and it didn't cost them a penny. It also meant we could employ specialists of our own to see our patients like Dermatologists and Physios and Rheumatologists. One day this nice old chap came to see me. He had a 'sausage' growing from his upper eyelid. This was very thin but was about 2cms long. Just in our short consultation it irritated me immensely, so I can only imagine what it was doing to the poor chap. I offered to refer him. It was about April. I sent a letter to the surgeons who told me they could not remove it as it needed the skills of an eye surgeon. I therefore referred him to the eye surgeons. The appointment was about nine months away. Our fund had a contract with an eye surgeon who saw him within two weeks and who removed it within six weeks.

The patient was delighted. What came next, however, was the most interesting. The eye surgeon wrote to me; he had put the sample under the microscope and there, right in the middle, was a tiny focus of cancerous cells. He told me that it was probably quite safe as it looked as though it had all been removed but, just to be sure, he would like to see the patient again. I therefore contacted the elderly gentleman and he came in to see me a few days later, I told him about the tiny cancer but that it was most likely quite safe. I informed him that I had booked a follow-up appointment for him for about 2 weeks' time.

He gripped my hand and said, "No, Doctor, you have spent quite enough on me. I thank you most sincerely, but it's time to spend on others." I told him that this was how the fund worked and there was enough to care for all the others too. He still refused to go back and would not hear of it but, fortunately, never had any further trouble from his eyes.

One day I walked into work and I noted that the next door building, the DSS office was for sale. I asked several colleagues if they thought it was time for us to move. Our Practice Nurse, Joan Lee, told me that she thought it was a brilliant idea and, there and then, we walked round it. I suggested to the other partners that it was a good time to move. Dr Broxton felt so strongly about the breathless pace of change that I'd driven forwards and felt that we were simply moving too quickly. She felt so strongly that she actually wrote to me. I just knew it was time and managed to bring her round. Our plans advanced steadily and she was a hard working and enthusiastic contributor – once her nerves had settled a bit! We did not move next door, however, as there were problems with the electrical substation, which we were told would cost a million pounds to move. I think it was moved when they put in the new car parks and knocked Eccles HC down! (no, I checked today it's still there!) As events came about, we found a super piece of land on Russell Street which was the site of the old Conservative club. This was a grand old Victorian house and the place where our car park is now was its lawns and bowling green. The plot of land was owned by Seddons the builders who told us that they would happily sell us the land as long as they could quote and build for what we had planned. I went to see Alan Campbell, Alan Berry and Evelyn Bridge at our local FHSA. They could not have been more helpful and also told me that they would like to help us with the project. We approached the RBS and, between us, borrowed a scary sum of money but we just carried on. We didn't look back and, soon after, we moved into wonderful accommodation where, at that time, we had oodles of space. Shortly afterwards Dr Tyrrell joined us from Monton and even more patients were under our roof.

Sadly, things were not going well between me and Lorraine. This was all my fault. I think they call it commitment phobia. We'd been going out for two years and I was aware that time was passing. She was a wonderful person and so many friends informed me, quite correctly, that she was devoted to me. I was really nervous about settling down; this in turn made her more unsettled and anxious, and the end result was that we ran into row after row. On paper we were great, and a nicer person one would struggle to come across. I was agonising over it for months and months and months. Just when I thought the answer was before me we'd have another row. Eventually, I reasoned that by making a commitment, the rows would disappear, so we got engaged. This made things even worse. The rows continued and we had several break-ups only to get back together again. Our mutual friends were amazing and did everything they could to get us back on track and to keep us there. They never took sides.

Of course I was still living at home with my mum, but had just bought a piece of land next door and had chosen an architect and builder. Construction was due to begin in Feb 1989. My Mum was really worried about me. She didn't dislike Lorraine at all, but could sense the turmoil which was not getting easier for me or for Lorraine. We'd parted so many times only for us to get back together again. One day in surgery Gladys came to see me. She was a nice lady but had always hinted that she could see what others could not. She had a habit of looking past you almost as though she could literally see something that was invisible to everyone else. We'd completed our consultation and then she said something to me that made me think that I had misheard her. First she said, "Your mum's been to see me." I thought I'd misheard. I said, "Pardon?" "Yes," she said, "your mum came to see me." I stared at her not knowing quite what to say. Then she said, "She is so worried about you." I said, "Pardon?"

She laughed at my shocked expression. "Yes," she said, "Your Mum's been to see me. I've told her not to worry about you. You are going to be okay." I didn't even know that Gladys knew my mum or vice versa which is was made me so unsettled. Gladys then told me that she could see my future and had told my mum what she wanted to know. She had that funny look on her face as she said it. I was speechless.

I am not sure if it was just before this, or just after, that I'd parted for the last time with Lorraine. I realised, to my shame, that it was only the day we split that I noticed the colour of her eyes. She decided to leave Manchester. She had a large leaving do at one of the very popular pizza places in town. I am told that there wasn't a dry eye in the place. My name was 'mud'. Though the nicest thing was that this was not from Lorraine, who never said bad things about me, although I suspect she had every right to. Sometimes songs will remind one of times in one's life and whenever I hear "Now those Days are Gone" by Bucks Fizz I think of this time.

I must confess as to being a bit sceptical about Gladys as I could simply not see what she could see and what, if anything, she could possibly have told my Mother! A year or two later Gladys became very ill and she was, sadly, dying. I visited her at home; she lived in an old Victorian house near the old fire station. As I was driving away, my tyre was ripped to shreds by a very unusual object almost like a metal dart. It was a funny thought that came to me, as I struggled with my spare tyre, that this was almost like a message sent to me from her, "Are you still sceptical?" She had, at that time, a lovely pottery shop on Liverpool Road, just near to the Patricroft Bridge. After she'd passed away, her daughter contacted me to say that she was clearing her mum's shop and was there anything I would like, as she was certain her mum would like me to have something. This, without doubt, was both humbling and touching. I did not like to turn up at their time of mourning and say, "Yes, I'd like this, please." Anyway, she sent for me a lovely vase with a Kingfisher on it. It's still on my shelf in my little study all these years later, and I think of Gladys and what was said between her and my Mum that day. I was also told that my Mum went to see Lorraine before she left but, again, I am not sure what was said.

A couple of weeks after Lorraine and I broke up, I approached Dr Jacobs, who was the course organiser for the new batch of GP trainees. One of my friends had moved to

Leicester and had started his own practice. He went on to achieve great success. He was an amazing doctor and very skilled. I remember on the Obstetrics and Gynaecology rotation we were doing 'lift out' forceps where the baby was already quite well down. He was doing Keilland's forceps where the baby would have to be rotated by the blades of the forceps in order to deliver it successfully through the birth canal. Any mistake and you could damage or kill the baby. We were doing minor procedures in theatre and he was doing much more complicated procedures. Not just this. I remember when I was doing Elderly Care medicine and he was in Casualty, any patients that he'd seen that were destined for me were all beautifully worked up, with detailed notes and also all the bloods done and waiting. He was also a big hit with the ladies. Lorraine's best friend, who held a bit of a torch for him, used to say about the stories associated with his name. "If just half of them were true, then it still left one with an awful lot to go off!"

It turned out that this doctor, Ali, was looking for a female business partner to join him in Leicester. I asked Eva if any of her class were planning to head south. She said that yes, there was one whose parents had moved to Leicester. I asked her if she would inform her. She told me that it was my job offer and I should arrange to see her myself. A week or two later Frances Webb came to see me in her little red-rimmed glasses and blue pleated skirt. She sat on my chair and we talked and talked and talked. She told me some time later that she could not understand why I had walked her back to her car. I guess that I didn't want her to leave. Something had hit me like a sledge hammer and I just knew that Frankie was the one. A week or two later I phoned her to ask if she would fancy coming out to dinner and would she like to check her diary? She told me that her schedule was empty and yes, that would be very nice. Something told me that she was the one: the right person at the right time.

Lorraine had heard that I had moved on and wrote to me to ask if this was something I had prepared in advance, as things had happened so quickly. I sent her a long, long letter, a copy of which I still have, and informed her that I had not met Frankie until two weeks after our last split. I also offered my unreserved apologies.

Six weeks later I was asking Frankie to marry me. She said that it was way too soon and I think she kept me waiting for about six months before I got an answer. We were away in North Wales and I asked her if she thought we should phone her parents to ask them if they were happy with us getting engaged or should we call it quits. She said, "Oh, no I don't think we should do that." We phoned her mum and dad that night and on the way back we stopped in Chester for an engagement ring. The song from this time is Carly Simon and "The Right Thing To Do." It's been 'our song' ever since.

Many, many year's later Lorraine's photo popped out of a drawer in my study and I was telling my two girls about my time with the most amazing midwife and about a relationship that we couldn't make work, mainly because of my failings. Lottie, who was about 15 at the time, looking very sad, asked me if Lorraine was okay. I couldn't say that I had had any contact with her but I certainly hoped so, as she didn't deserve to be anything else.

The house was finished, just about, and a week after we were married we moved in. We are still there and our girls are both at University doing their finals. Time has gone by so quickly. My mum was getting older. She was diagnosed as having breast cancer. I am sure she must have told her GP that she didn't want referring. In any event, he started her on medication that might just have shrunk the tumour, but when she did not go back for any more he neither contacted her nor me to warn me. I am not sure how he could have neglected her as either a patient or the mother of one of his colleagues but, anyway, there we are. She had a horrible death as the cancer became very vigorous. Her house was just at the bottom of our garden and she died in 1996. She is buried near my Dad, in accordance with her wishes. Before she died she said something to me that still rings in my ears to this day. She said, "John, you are a wonderful, kind person. You have a lovely way with people and please try to keep this up over the years, even when people and events sometimes make it difficult." I try my best to run to this each and every day. We took Lottie back to University in Newcastle some months ago and she was a bit shaky. I told her the words that my Mum had said to me and I now wanted to say them to her.

Of course dads are very proud of their girls and I am no exception. I remember walking back from school with them both when they were both very young. Emily kicked, by accident, an empty plastic bottle that had been thrown on the pavement. She picked it up without any words from me and carried it 50 yards to the next bin. Then there was an incident on the ski train that I will tell you about later.

The other incident which makes me think that Emily will be a super doctor was a very simple thing that happened when we were walking up Rivington Pike one Sunday. An elderly gentleman was standing completely still, just staring at his coat that was on the ground. I thought to myself that he must have had an 'event' like a tiny stroke or even a mini-fit. The interesting thing was that, without any words from me Emily went up to him and said, “Excuse me, Sir, forgive me for troubling you and I hope you don’t mind me asking, but are you feeling okay? Can I help you in any way?” Emily had just entered fourth year at this time and she already had the look and feel and concern for her fellow men that will stand her in good stead. Emily phoned us a few weeks ago to say that some of the students had been given ‘yellow forms’. She told us that these were given to those who were in danger of failing their finals. We waited with bated breath while she told us that she had not been given one, but had been given a blue form for those who were doing really well. Only one or two were given out. She texted us a copy and some wonderful things were written about her by her tutors. She and Lottie are due to finish this June and Frankie and I will be in the front row cheering them both on. I’d like to think that although my Dad did not make my graduation, he will be there with us cheering too.

Many years ago, when both girls were young, a lady used to call occasionally to ask us if we wanted to buy any of her artwork. To be truthful we were so hard up that we could only do this once or twice over a few years. One night she was leaving and it was cold and raining cats and dogs. Lottie went to the door with her and asked her if she had a car.

The woman snapped at Lottie thinking she was being materialistic. “Oh, of course I have a car.” What she missed was that Lottie was concerned about her braving the elements if she was on foot, and was simply asking out of concern in the way that someone might ask if you have an umbrella on a rainy day. She disappeared into the night oblivious to a little girl’s concern for her.

Several of my patients expressed surprise that I did not want a boy. We were very happy with what we were given. There were three Magpies on the roof before we had Emily and three on the roof before we had Charlotte. More than this, before we had Emmie there was a programme on telly about the 'dying rooms' in China where girl babies are effectively discarded. Then, before Lottie arrived there was a programme on the telly about how in India female foetuses are aborted at a very early age, as soon as the scan can detect their sex. Frankie and I reasoned that we'd be very grateful for two girls who we'd do our very best to love and to look after.

Although we had moved in to our house just next door to my Mum's, we had two carpets in the whole place, a bed, a second-hand sofa and a small dining table. My Mum was constantly asking us to let her help with furniture. One day she said she had bought something from a furniture shop in Eccles that she'd had to take back. They had given her a credit note and she was going to give it to us and would not take no for an answer. The furniture shop came and fitted a beautiful wool carpet in our lounge which, although a pale lilac colour, was magnificent and was down for over 15 years. Within twelve months of moving in mortgage interest rates had gone crazy and for a few weeks were about 16%. I was destitute and Frankie was pregnant and had had to give up her work. A man was driving past with a large van. He looked at the bare, clay soil and said he had 3 bags of manure left on his van and he only wanted 60p each for them. He told me that they would be perfect to dig into the depleted soil. I told him that I did not want them. He thought I was being 'sniffy' not wanting his manure. What he did not realise was that I did not have £1.80 to give him and it had nothing to do with being standoffish. Such financial penury lasted for most of our early married years, but, slowly, we bought another carpet or two and some furniture.

In the early days of our marriage we couldn't afford to go away. After a year or two however, we found that travelling to Jersey was inexpensive and we engaged in some great holiday pursuits with our girls such as rock pooling and flying kites on the beach – simple pleasures. In the fullness of time we were able to go further afield and in 2001 we went with a female colleague, and her young family, to Florida. This was an amazing, exciting holiday. I remember one afternoon we'd just got to the MGM park. There getting out of his 4x4 entering the Boardwalk hotel was a famous tennis player. Our friend immediately took off across the car park running towards him. "Mr Borg", she said, "Mr Borg!" She raced across the car park determined to meet up with him, continually calling his name.

I raced after her as quickly as I could, shouting after her as loudly as I was able, "No, that's not Bjorn Borg, it's Boris Becker!" Mercifully the famous tennis player scurried quickly inside the hotel before embarrassment descended all round!

I mentioned above about the attractive young woman on the train. You will all know, won't you, that things come full circle? At least some things do. At that moment, it's then up to us to make of them what we will. Ultimately I guess we judge ourselves. One episode, of I hope many, sticks in my mind. We were in Wengen skiing. It was probably late December. Frankie, the girls and I were sitting on the little train that takes about half an hour to take you to the ski lifts and then, if you wish, to the top of the mountain.

It is always busy at such times and we were all relieved to have found seats. Lots of people would be piling on and there would be little standing room very shortly. Remember too, that although it's cold up there the train is heated and everyone has their ski gear on including fleeces, ski jackets and gloves, helmets etc. There was one seat remaining in our carriage. Most skiers are, as you might expect, young and fit. The lady who then got on was much older and looked a little unsteady on her feet. I looked at the vacant seat. I kept thinking to myself, "Just sit down before someone else takes that seat!" Recently, I was reading a book about compassion. It held that showing compassion to others also feeds back and helps oneself. I won't lie, I was thinking if she didn't sit down and had no seat then I was going to have to stand all the way up that mountain! She sat down and I breathed an inward sigh of relief. What happened next blew me away. A gentleman, even more elderly, got on and stood next to her. He was even more infirm. He was her husband. She then stood up and gave him her seat just as more started piling on. The train was about to depart.

I knew the game was up. I could no more have let the older woman stand than fly to the moon. I stood up and offered her my seat. Just in this moment both Emmie and Lottie, without being asked, stood up. One of them said to me. 'No, Dad this one's on us." This was a double bonus. It showed not only had I been happy to give up my seat but, hopefully, by example over the years, my girls had witnessed such things and were prepared to give up theirs. The lady sat down next to me. My French isn't bad. I caught the gist of what she was saying; that my girls had been very kind and had set a good example. In my broken French I said to her that we did our best but that perhaps English people were not well regarded in the world today. She emphatically shook her head as if to say she would not hear and could not agree with such a thing.

The following day a couple passed me at great speed going down a steep icy, red run. It was the elderly couple who could obviously ski better than they could walk!

Occasionally one can turn the arguments around. One day in another ski resort we were waiting for the little train to take us up the mountain. One French chap in broken English was berating this Scottish lady with two lads for pushing in. For perhaps the only time in my life I summoned perfect French and reminded him that 2 minutes before she had arrived he had pushed in front of our group. The same holiday we were coming down on the train and two youths were sitting on seats near us. They had their wet ski boots on and had put them on the facing train seats, I looked sharply at them and said aloud, "I just hope you are not English!"

You may wonder what a chap is doing skiing when he nearly lost his right arm at eleven? When we got married, Frankie was a keen skier and had her own skis and boots. She asked me if we could go skiing. I told her that she must be mad, or I would be mad to risk my arm in this way. She accepted my decision, somewhat reluctantly. Many years later when Emmie was at senior school she asked us if she could go on the school ski trip and we said that she could. When the time came to pick her up she got off the coach parked outside the school. She looked fabulous and also said that she'd had a wonderful time. I said to Frankie that I'd been hasty, we had to get into skiing. Moreover M&S at that time were offering ski-wear. I bought a ski jacket at less than half price, £20. I told Frankie that it must be a sign.

I think it must have been the following year or maybe later the same year we flew on a little propeller plane called an APT to Switzerland. My air-hostess friend says they are known as "All Passengers Terrified" but I must say that it was amazing and were in the little car-free village of Wengen, just before Christmas Eve. This was a magical village and Christmas Eve there was a service in the village chapel in English. It was packed and the skier sat next to the snowboarder in the little chapel as the clanking central-heating pipes did their best to warm the hundreds who'd squeezed in. There was very little snow but my ski instructor told me that it would ski that night. As we walked back from the service to the hotel, there began a deluge of snow. The flakes seemed massive and I have a picture of both our girls walking with their mum through the snow-covered village.

By day I was doing my best to learn to ski. It was hard going but by the end of the week I could do simple and gentle runs, with some fear but largely remaining upright. Since then we have really got into it and, although the girls are amazing and elegant skiers, I can just about keep up but don't have anywhere near as smooth an action as they. Last March Frankie and I journeyed to Selva and took a day trip to Cortina. One of the runs here is known as the James Bond run as they set one of the films here. You can also find designer ski lifts, ones that have been sponsored by designer houses such as Paul & Shark. There is also to be found the Women's downhill championship course, which is not that long but is incredibly steep. Our rep asked us to split into two groups; those who wanted to take the gentler slope down and those who wanted to try the women's downhill. I must have been mad but I elected to try the championship slope. At the top looking down I was terrified. I had skied down part of the way, which was really steep. I stood next to the rep and looked down – it was a sheer drop. I looked back up the slope and realised that it was too steep to walk back up. Suddenly, the rep skied down. I was standing on my own. I knew the more I hesitated the more frightened I would become. I have never been on anything so steep in my life. I knew it was now or never. I started skiing across the slope. At the edge of the slope two people had fallen and two had taken their skis off and were trying to walk down. It was too steep to walk down! They looked petrified. As I went across I knew that I had to turn. This was the moment when the skis would look straight down the slope and missing the turn or falling would mean that I would head straight down at an ever-increasing speed. If I could just put that first turn in then I could do another and so on. I offloaded the skis and began the turn. To my amazement I had completed the turn and was still upright and in control. I then continued to put more turns in and within a few seconds I was down. I then looked back up the slope. The two in our group who had come behind me had both fallen. They immediately fell at least 30 feet and could not stop. One of them tried to stand up half way down but it was impossible. It was simply too steep. If they had gone ahead of me and promptly fallen there was no way I could have continued.

It seems that one minute I am moaning about my arm and the next taking daredevil risks. The truth lies in what happened when I was young. It may have been the swimming and my efforts to find an excuse each week. I hated myself for this and I knew that excuses and avoidance did not make the fear go away, it multiplies it. One has to face the fear and just get on with it. There is no alternative and this run was simply a way of my doing that. I realise, however, that there is a fine line between this and recklessness. I leave you to judge. I bumped into a member of our group who had taken the easier route down. He told me that he was a Police firearms instructor and he couldn't risk taking a fall and being unable to work. I looked a bit sheepish but did not reply.

The other point of note is that it is essential that one keeps physically fit. Too many people, especially those of a certain age, wander on to the slopes and expect to shoot down really steep slopes after a couple of lessons. It's a punishing environment up there. In Canada for instance it was minus 30 centigrade. I saw a lady whilst coming down a slope with two young children, neither of who had either hats or gloves. If I'd seen them sooner I would have stopped and advised the silly woman that her children were at risk of frostbite at best and losing fingers at worst!

Sadly too, some young people especially lads can be reckless. We were coming down a slope one day in our group of skiers all having a lesson. Two really tall lads shot down the slope using snow blades. These are like skis but much smaller. They were coming down without regard to less experienced skiers or the young. Our ski instructor went after them, stopped them and informed them that if she saw them again doing such reckless things, then she would take their ski passes off them which would mean that they would be unable to get back up the mountain.

Please note, I have no wish to scare myself. You won't find me eating any butter beans and I have trouble cutting back the weeds when frogs start hopping out. At such times I usually go and find Frankie so that she can come and move them for me. However, this being said, if I am confronted directly by something that terrifies me then I have to face it. I remember an incident when Frankie was pregnant, a patient came in who was bright yellow. Infective and blood-borne jaundice can be easily transmitted. The patient needed urgent blood tests to rule out things like Hepatitis and Cancer. A little finger prick of the needle that I used to take his blood in those days before routine vaccination could have gone badly for me and also for Frankie. I knew that I could ask one of the nurses to take the bloods for me, but I could not ask them to somehow shield me from risk. It was my job to step up. I took the bloods and sorted the patient who later recovered beautifully.

My other penchant for going down steep things very quickly is the water slide. One year we went to Wet 'n Wild in Florida. There are two very high and very steep water slides. Bomb Bay is a capsule that one enters and one then waits for the operator to operate it basically by the floor opening below. My preferred option was Der Stuka which is just as high and just as steep but one can decide when one sets off. This suited me and though once again I was terrified, I knew that I just had to do it. As one goes down the slide it seems really steep so much so that it is important to lean back so one's body does not fall forwards out of the slide, yes it is that steep! A few seconds later and one enters the deceleration trough. At this point one notices that the pockets in one's swim shorts have 'blown out' and one's hair, yes I had hair in those days, was standing on end with the speed of decent. Heady stuff and not something I'd be keen to repeat these days!

Before leaving the subject of holidays, I want to tell you about my first holiday without my parents. Carol and I ventured to Larnaca, Cyprus some time in the early 80s. It was a very different island in those days and I remember Ayia Napa was a deserted fishing village! We ate each night in the hotel restaurant and guests sat at the same table each night. A couple sat at a nearby table during our stay.

Each night the chap would stand on his chair and then on the table. His partner would watch as he then proceeded to poke the light fitting above their table with either his knife or his fork. I was spellbound watching this scenario each night. The tables had circular seats around them and in the ceiling above the circular theme would be continued in the light fittings which were of a circular configuration to match the seating in the restaurant. On the floor above was the bar area and once again in this room there were circular seats which corresponded to the circular light fittings in the restaurant below.

I became absolutely fascinated watching this scenario play out each night. One evening, in the bar, I realised we were sitting in the seats directly above their table. Below our seats would be the light fitting that he had been prodding with his fork for several days. I got on my hands and knees and looked under the table and the circular seats to see if there was anything that might give me a clue as to what he was doing. I was racking my brains. I wondered if the light fitting was faulty and he was prodding it with his fork in an attempt to fix it in some way. I reasoned that not even I would be so stupid as to do something like that by prodding a live light with a metal fork!

Night after night I would ask Carol what he could possibly be doing. We became more and more puzzled as the holiday went on. He would spend a long time actually standing on the table while his wife looked on, prodding the light with his cutlery.

My answer came a few days later. I realised that the couple had departed and their table was empty. Here was my chance! I looked up at the circular light fitting which had several bulbs mounted above a circular sheet of frosted glass which provided illumination. I could see nothing. Carol stood next to me and we just stared upwards. I just had to know. I took my shoes off and stood on the chair, the one the gentleman sat in. He would stand on this then on the table and his prodding would begin. I stood on the chair now a lot closer to the light fitting above. I could tell that the frosted glass was circular and had a rim round its edge. There was a gap between the rim and the circular border that framed the light fitting and then was carried on through the ceiling to make up the circular benches in the bar upstairs. At first I could see nothing. Then as I reached up holding my arms above my head out of frustration something moved in the gap and a pair of beady eyes looked down. There staring at me was a beautiful black and white pussycat, calmly waiting for his tea to be fed to him! He had obviously found a way into the light fitting by crawling under the seats in the bar above. Sadly, his friend and sponsor had gone home!

CHAPTER XII

2am Surgery

Things at the Health Centre were going from strength to strength, especially when we moved to St Andrews. I found myself in the midst of some wonderful colleagues, staff and, of course, patients. Friends would sometimes ask me if I would prefer to work in somewhere like Wilmslow or some other posh area. I could never want this. Working amongst the people that I grew up with was just about perfect and such folk made for kind, generous and, at times when things had gone wrong, forgiving patients. I wouldn't ever have wanted to work anywhere else.

On a fairly regular basis I would manage to get myself in a pickle. On one occasion a patient trapped me in my room and insisted that I look at his genitals as the hospital appointment had not come through yet. He would not let me leave the room. My receptionists had phoned the police but my practice nurse, Marie Rowson, who was petite even by my standards, insisted on barging in and stood between him and me telling him as she pointed an accusatory finger at him that he was being an aggressive bully and he should be ashamed of himself.

One patient became very paranoid whenever he had a chest infection. I visited him at home and realised he had pneumonia. I asked the hospital to admit him. This they did and also put a drip up containing powerful antibiotics. That night he realised that he didn't want to be in hospital and absconded from the ward. He then took a bus home, wearing just his dressing gown and pyjamas. He wheeled the drip and metal stand through Eccles and even took it with him on the bus. The hospital phoned us in a state of panic wondering where he was.

Then there was the patient who'd been told some years before by an orthopaedic surgeon that she should rest her bad back. She had taken his advice literally and had gone to her bed while her poor husband ferried a constant stream of food, drink, puzzle books, library books and, of course, cigarettes to her smooth and unruffled eiderdown. I went in there and suggested that she get out of bed and come for a little walk with me. I charged down the side of the bed and started to move the wicker chair so she would have more room. Only the slight sloshing sound warned me as I hoisted it aloft. Mercifully for me, it was raining and I had pulled the belt on my mac a bit tighter than usual. I realised too late that the chair was really a commode, which was full, and my mac was covered almost as completely as my embarrassment did me. What was nice, however, was the genuine concern that the elderly couple showed me that day.

One night on-call I'd been called to an elderly gentleman who had wandered into his neighbour's house saying that his brother, with whom he lived, had stopped taking to him. I went and met him at the neighbour's. As we walked back to the patient's house, it transpired that he had not spoken for a week or two. My fears rose steadily at the true fate of the elder brother. We walked to this large Victorian detached house in Ellesmere Park which was all in complete darkness. The neighbour had a large torch but as soon as we approached the big house he disappeared and went back home – along with his torch! As I walked with the elderly gentleman the answers to my questions made me increasingly uneasy. It seemed that not only had he stopped speaking, he had not eaten or drunk anything or in fact moved for some days! We went in through the front door which opened only a little bit, just enough for me to squeeze through. I wondered if the poor older brother was dead behind the door. The door closed behind me; it was pitch black. The elderly chap then asked me to wait there and scurried off into the distance. I could not see a thing.

Worse still was that I could not move. It was so narrow that I had to turn my case sideways just to fit in the gap and then realised I could not move forwards. It was as though I was pinned against the front door. After some minutes with increasingly wild thought going through my head a light came on somewhere in the back of the house. I could see that there was a gigantic pile of furniture stacked as high as the lofty ceiling. High above me I could just make out a stained glass cupola which must have given light to the hall but the whole thing, stairs and all was filled to capacity with furniture all neatly tied with corrugated paper and string. The elderly gentleman called to me to follow the light and in due course I found the little back room containing two beds and a kitchen sink. On the far bed the older brother had been dead for some time. Mercifully my concern for the younger brother banished all my fears and I broke it to him that his brother had passed away some days before. He nodded but did not seem unduly surprised. The brother told me that the two of them were the last survivors of a thriving family business selling furniture in Eccles. When the business failed their father had brought all the remaining stock home and had it all stacked in the large house.

A few days later I was chatting to the undertaker. He told me that they had had to strap the deceased to a stretcher and carry the body vertically through the narrow passageway. A few weeks later I heard that the surviving brother had also passed away. I am told they cleared the house in less than 24 hours. I couldn't help but wonder how long it had taken to stack it all in the first place.

You will find many of these tales in my books. They are all true and can only be told with patient consent or after they have passed away. My favourite, however, is not about a patient at all. It was a cold Sunday afternoon in October and I was on call. The family were not my patients and I had not met them before. It was a little terraced house in Salford: literally a two-up, two-down. The front door opened directly into the living room. I had been called to see a little boy who was poorly. Doctors scan a room and the patient very quickly, looking for clues as to how and why they are ill. As the door opened I saw the little boy sitting on the sofa next to his mum and a brother or a sister.

I went into the room. I saw that there was a roaring coal fire. On the rug in front of the fire was a pig, all pink and spotty. It was still sleeping and had not stirred on my entering the room.

I said, "Oh, there's a pig!"

The lady's eyes went to the ceiling, she had obviously heard this so many times and she smiled a little indulgently and nodded, "Yes, it is a pig."

Not just any pig, but an absolutely enormous pig. It had the pink skin with the black spots and was quietly snoring away as it slumbered in front of this roaring fire.

I was filled with questions. "What was it doing there, where did it sleep, was it a pet, were they as intelligent as people said, how did they get it, were they keeping it for a farmer?"

I think the poor lady wondered if her little boy was ever going to be seen.

Just as my questions reached their height the pig woke up and looked round and promptly went back to sleep again.

The lady told me that it was a family pet. They'd bought it as a miniature pig that would only grow a little. Then it grew and grew and grew. It was intelligent and made a good pet despite its size. They did not have the heart to give it away or sell it as they had grown fond of it.

This was typical of local folk. They would never have wanted to part with their pig and family pet despite the difficulties of keeping such a large animal in a small house with a young family.

Occasionally, as you've seen, we'd have the odd aggressive or violent patient. Such cases were thin on the ground and even those who were known to be violent would often be very well behaved in the doctor's surgery. Even when I was trapped by the patient in my room I did not feel in any danger. Although all the rooms have panic buttons, I cannot remember a time when one has been activated because a doctor was in danger. A situation that can go badly awry is when a patient is mentally ill. I was called one day by social services. A young mother had barricaded herself into her house with two tiny children. She had had a psychotic breakdown and was convinced that the radiators were controlling her thoughts. Social services were planning to section her and remove her physically, if need be, in order to protect the children. When I got there it was like something out of Dragnet. The road was blocked; there were Police, an Ambulance, social services and tens of neighbours. I knew the lady. I went in and, mercifully, she agreed to come out with me. Although this was a potentially nasty situation, of course social services and the police have to act if they feel the children or patient are in danger. That lady is so much better today, her children are all grown up and, to this day, she is always so pleasant and friendly towards me at all times.

I mentioned above that things turn; they have a habit of coming full circle. I have found this through much of my life, I'm sure like so many people. How we react or handle these occasions is significant and I do try to 'rise' to these events. I was called out to see a man who was in agony on the floor. He had a terrible pain going down his back and into his legs. I suspected that he had a nasty slipped disc and thought he was going to have to go into hospital. I phoned Hope and asked if the Orthopaedic Surgeon could do an urgent domiciliary visit to see the chap and admit him. In those days such visits were not unusual. I had trouble getting through to the consultant. Meanwhile the patient's wife had become so worried about him that she'd phoned an ambulance and promptly saved his life. The real diagnosis was a ruptured aortic aneurysm. With such a diagnosis the patient, if untreated, may only have minutes left to live. In the event, he was admitted and operated upon and lived for many years. The consultant wrote to me; he'd heard that I was trying to get hold of him and he was unhappy because he always carried an emergency bleep (this was in the days before mobile phones!) and was always contactable. I wrote to him to apologise. The person at fault was I and I alone. There was no way he should assume any blame whatsoever and I bore full responsibility for any confusion and mix up. I also told him that I would be especially troubled if he had been made to worry about what was my error. I then reminded Mr Green of the little boy's arm he'd saved that night. I said that I was more grateful than my words could convey that he had done so and that I thought about him not only every time I use it, but also of his sense of duty in coming in off his holiday in order to save my shattered arm.

It used to be said that doctors should never apologise; that you'd be letting yourself in for a lot of trouble if the case came to court and it would count against you. I think this is poppycock and if something has gone wrong, as of course it does from time to time, then one owes the patient an apology that they most surely deserve. It at least gives the patient some satisfaction that the doctor has learned from his mistake and acknowledges the patient's trauma or that of their relatives. My Mum's GP apologised to me that he had not been more on the ball and had not been more diligent. Although I was disappointed in him because I thought he was a better GP than he turned out to be, making a song and dance was not going to bring her back.

I remember a gentleman who had a very unusual lesion on his shoulder. It was so big and looked horrible. I remember thinking that if it was a malignant melanoma then it would most surely have killed him by then. I referred him but, unfortunately, not with an urgent priority. He was seen and, as you would expect, the specialist can only prioritise appointments by what the GP tells him. Anyway, it turned out to be a malignant melanoma which was not only very wide but also very deep (the worst indicator for such a thing). I saw him before he died and told him that I wanted to apologise to him for my routine referral which had taken 6 weeks when he should in retrospect have been seen within 2 weeks. He held out his hand to shake mine and said that I wasn't to worry as when I'd seen him it looked a lot less angry and had not started to bleed. His kindness and forgiveness to me that day humbled me.

I suspect that like many GPs and doctors in general, I have a 2 am surgery where cases are gone through in my head – cases where things could'a, would'a, should'a been different if only I'd done that blood test, referred the patient a bit sooner, realised that they would not take the tablets or that they would take them all. This is the price to be paid for being the man in the chair and I stand by my responsibilities. When I was working full-time I would usually see 650 patients each and ever month. I would also work nearly every night until midnight for many years. You can see that just the occasional thing going wrong can cause mayhem.

Losing a patient that we have known for some time is never easy and sometimes we cry with the relatives too. I go past houses that so-and-so used to live in and sometimes I visit new families in houses that I have been in before where that nice patient used to live. I remember one nice lady who was feeling very tired. She had had some bloods done only six months before. I suggested we re-ran them and I sent off another sample. That afternoon the lab phoned me to tell me that it was grossly abnormal. The poor lady had a really aggressive leukaemia. She was not particularly old. She was not on the telephone, so I went to her home to see if she was in. She opened the door and saw me standing there. No words were spoken just in that moment, but her face fell as she read the concern on my face. I felt like the Angel of Death standing there on her doorstep. I told her that I was sorry to present in this way but her blood test was not right and I wondered if I could admit her to hospital immediately. The poor soul nodded and went to hospital where she was kept in. She died two weeks later without ever coming home.

It always amazes me how tough some patients are, especially those of a certain age. One gentleman came in and asked me if I'd look at a scratch that he had on his arm. As he took off his jacket a massive ulcer was revealed that was down to the bone and must have been there for months. I nearly fell off my chair when I looked at it. I phoned one elderly lady to tell her that I needed her to go to hospital as her bloods were dangerously out of balance. She told me that this was impossible as she had flights to Tenerife that afternoon. I did manage, barely, to convince her that attending hospital was the smart thing to do and that there would be most likely many more holidays to come, which there were.

Patients are not only forgiving they are also unfailingly kind. One Christmas I was given 30 bottles of whisky. Well, it can now be revealed that I very rarely drink. I have lost too many patients to drink and to be truthful it does not entice me at all – apart from the odd lager shandy. I remember in giving those thirty bottles away I suddenly had lots of good friends! One elderly gentleman insisted on buying me a bottle each Christmas. I said to him one year that this was too expensive a gift and perhaps he could just get me a can of lager. The following Christmas he bought me 24 cans of lager as well as a bottle of whisky. As part of my revalidation I had to seek at least one-hundred questionnaires from patients. These were anonymous and given out at the front desk. I was amazed and humbled by some of the kind comments that were made, comments that I will treasure for always.

Living locally meant that I could always nip out and see poorly patients. Many times on a Sunday when Frankie was cooking the tea I would pop out and visit a terminal patient. It was nice to see the surprise on their faces when I turned up. They were also eternally grateful. I remember at the time of the Queen's Jubilee there were two Bank Holidays, one either side of a weekend. I saw this elderly lady with a nasty pneumonia. I asked her to let me admit her but she refused. I thought she would be dead by the end of the weekend. I visited her three times and by the Monday morning she was already improving. She and her husband still come in to see me.

So, as my professional career draws to a close, I look back with great respect and admiration for the staff and colleagues I have been fortunate to work with. I'm also grateful to the two young doctors who decided to join me when Dr Lindsay retired. They surely had big shoes to fill. NHS England warned me that they would close the list and disperse all the patients across Eccles if I was not able to find a partner to work with me – so I am, without doubt, indebted to them for doing so.

As you have seen, my Dad's journey began 6000 miles away and not far off one hundred years ago. His origins date much further back and even longer ago than that. One of the greatest compliments paid to me is when my patients tell me that I am like Doctor Borkin. You will see a little plaque in reception just above the pay phone, (that isn't working!)

dedicated to Dr Borkin. An even greater compliment, if such a thing is possible, is when a patient tells me that I am so like my father. I would very much like him to think, that although the road has not at all always been smooth, it has been one that has helped many more than it has hindered and, at all times, it has been a privilege and an honour to be amongst such good colleagues and especially the patients to whom this book is dedicated. At all times it has been a wonderful experience and I am truly blessed to have been given the opportunity to serve, and carry out such work, amongst such great people. As I move to my own retirement I will think of so many of them and always look back fondly. It would be nice to think that my Dad has been with me on this journey and that his success has been my success, and vice versa.

This book, then, is also in large part about two men: Dr Borkin and my father. It was their example that I have endeavoured to follow to set my own professional pathway. Where this has been a success is largely due to them and where it has failed, then, this is where, for whatever reason, I had not applied or had forgotten to apply their way of working to the patient, case or problem in hand and, without doubt, responsibility for such a thing rests solely with me.

Of course I'd love to be able to say that this torch will be handed to my two girls but I know that their pathway is theirs and in many ways I'd like them to live, work and grow in an unencumbered way, devoid of the forces that made me and certainly of those that forged me from times of fear.

Both Emmie and Lottie went through finals this year. We had two graduations in two days in two cities. We were determined we'd be there cheering them on and we were lucky to be near the front of the audience in both. Emmie started work at the end of July. She was on-call her first weekend and became very tired. She phoned us to say that she hated it; she was a rubbish doctor and was no doubt going to do very badly. We just asked her to hang on and surely things could only improve. We are pleased to say that she is a lot more settled and due her first pay cheque any day. No doubt she will celebrate. Lottie has had a very different journey. She decided against medicine, as I don't think she wanted the slog.

She started Biomedical Science at Newcastle. After second year she said that she was unhappy and was thinking of packing it all in and doing Physiotherapy in London. This sounded very expensive. I suggested she try a year in industry. She applied for such a year at Mondelez, who now own Cadburys, in Reading. She went down got through the interviews and was awarded the job for a year. They paid her but she had to sort her own digs out. She quite enjoyed this and especially so the chocolate tasting course which she had to try out for. She was told that she was a good enough taster to take part and every time she tasted chocolate they paid her £20! She also managed to get into the staff shop and bought large Toblerones, also owned by Mondelez, for low prices. Lottie was undecided about lab work and went back to Newcastle and finished her final year. She was not sure what she wanted to do. At the university jobs fair she bumped into a chap from an Internet start up. He asked her if she would go through an informal telephone interview. They then asked her to be interviewed by the boss in America by Skype and then called her to the offices in Newcastle for a third and more intense interview where the CEO Skyped in from America. She was delighted to be offered the job as she has been very happy in Newcastle. She starts there next week and although none of us know much about it, she too, will be earning and she is very excited about the opportunity.

You'll be pleased to know that I toned down my Dad's idiosyncrasies when speaking to our girls. I might go on about a proper education and still have a penchant for seeing where things are made but I have done my best to make sure that they grow up to make their own minds up about things. It seems quaint now to talk of such things as national pride, or of someone who strove daily to be more and more like the people among whom he had come to live; someone who was full of both gratitude and admiration for those who had allowed him to live in a country that was very different from the one from which he had departed.

It seems completely at variance with the prevailing national mood that we should ever again think of ourselves as a great nation; a nation whose contribution to each other, to the world and to those who came from foreign lands wanting to become the same kind of person with the same values and attitudes, could ever be thought of as something that no other country could quite match.

I appreciate that in the 30 plus years since my Dad died, much has changed. My wish, as I mentioned at the beginning, would be simple – that just for one day if English people were able to see themselves through his eyes. I think this perspective would restore, refresh and invigorate a nation that has become inured to the belief that not only is our best time behind us but also that such a 'golden era' must surely have been one that was an entirely false construct made up by little Englanders who shot Mel Gibson while he was trying to recover the Enigma machine! Must it be that our view of ourselves and that of others towards us, together with our standing in a dysfunctional world, is the one that we deserve with dreadful items on the news and dire current events. My Dad would beg to differ and this story began the day when HMS Hood, the most beautiful battle cruiser that the world had ever seen, raised steam in her boilers and journeyed from Scapa Flow over 6,000 miles to totally impress a little boy who wondered just who were the magnificent people who had sent such a thing.

I know that he would be saddened by the things that one hears regularly on the news that we have all become accustomed to. We can no longer build nuclear reactors without French expertise and Chinese money. We need others to build railway tracks, locomotives for us and also passenger planes. We can, maybe, manage a few engines and a wing or two but not much more. We could certainly, no longer build a 16-inch naval gun let alone a turret to put it in or a warship to fire it. I read a book once that stated that Britain used to have two full-time battleship salesmen!

In many ways this is a side argument, my Dad would always view the country and its people as the stuff of wonder that is very much still alive today if one knows where to look and does not spend too long on looking to the past.

He would have regarded himself at all times to be a lucky man among such people as the people of Britain and Manchester in particular. He and I would share these thoughts. He would certainly agree with me that discovering such things, and working with such folk, has meant the pleasure has been all mine. As I depart from a profession that has influenced me so much and given me such pleasure, I realise that it is now time to close my 2 am surgery. I hope that you all know that I will be thinking of you at all times and wish for each and every one of you health and happiness.

With my thanks and best wishes to you all.

Oops, nearly forgot, a couple of songs you might like:
One old - The Korgis “Don’t Look Back”.
One new - Basia Bulat “Someday Soon” – enjoy!

John Behardien